ADULT •
ERVISION
QUIRED

CONTENTS

Published 2011. Pedigree Books Ltd, Beech Hill House, Walnut Gardens, Exeter, Devon EX4 4DH books@pedigreegroup.co.uk | www.pedigreebooks.com

Pedigree®

£12.99

MEET THE GRIFFINS

Welcome to Quahog, Rhode Island and the 2012 Family Guy Annual. Whether you think you know everything there is to know about the Griffins and their friends, or if you're new to television's most anarchic animated comedy, this book is brimming with Family Guy fun about the most insane family on TV.

If you're easily offended leave now. But if you're up for jokes about pop culture, ding-a-lings and general nuttiness, then delve inside and say hello to Peter, Lois, Meg, Chris, Stewie and Brian.

PETER GRIFFIN

"WELL, EXCUSE ME FOR BEING RETARDED!"

Despite being a suburban father of three, Peter Löwenbräu Griffin has never had what you could call a normal life. Raised as the son of the strict Catholic Francis and his more relaxed mother, Thelma, it was only after his pops died that he discovered his real dad was a drunken Irishman called Mickey McFinnigan, who his mother had a brief fling with.

That isn't the only thing his mom kept from him. After decades of believing he was a proud American, Peter discovered he wasn't a US citizen at all. He was actually born in Mexico where his mother had originally planned to have an abortion.

You'd have thought he might have figured something fishy was going on during his youth - especially when his stepdad constantly told him that he wasn't his father. But Peter's not exactly the sharpest tack in the box. Indeed he's officially mentally retarded!

Despite all this, Peter bagged himself the beautiful and rich Lois Pewterschmidt as his wife and became the proud father of

two kids. He's also the somewhat reluctant dad of Meg too - and the father of Bertram, the result of a mishap at a sperm bank.

With his rather relaxed attitude to work, he's been through many jobs. In the early days of Family Guy he worked in a toy factory, until his boss, Mr. Weed, died and the factory was knocked down. Then he became a fisherman, helped by trusty Portuguese deckhands. Unfortunately his boat - the gloriously named 'S.S. More Powerful Than Superman, Batman, Spider-Man, and the Incredible Hulk Put Together' - got wrecked.

That led him to what he initially thought would be his dream job, working at the Pawtucket Patriot brewery. Sadly, he's stuck in the shipping department, constantly put down by his boss, Angela, who thinks he's a worse worker than Opie, who can't even talk.

DID YOU KNOW?

Peter's middle name, Löwenbräu, is a type of German beer, which translates as 'lion's brew'

He's also been a maid, bartender, school board president, tobacco lobbyist, erotic book author, policeman, president of his own country, renaissance fair jouster and even had to spend some time being Death.

Peter's life is filled with the bizarre, from an ongoing feud with a giant chicken to being in a barbershop quartet that breaks it to people that they have AIDS. It may be an unusual existence, but mostly Peter is just a Family Guy. ◾

LOIS GRIFFIN

"PETER, I CARE AS MUCH ABOUT THE SIZE OF YOUR PENIS AS YOU CARE ABOUT THE SIZE OF MY BREASTS."

Who wouldn't want to be born into a world of wealth and privilege? Well, Lois Griffin wasn't that keen on being from a wealthy background.

Despite being the child of ridiculously wealthy industrialist, Carter Pewterschmidt, and his wife, Barbara, Lois had a wild streak in her youth. Indeed, she starred in a skin flick to get money for drugs, and was so promiscuous that KISS star Gene Simmons knew her in his youth as 'Loose Lois'.

She met Peter Griffin during a visit to her rich Aunt Marguerite house, where he was employed by Marguerite as a towel boy.

Their budding romance was nearly destroyed by her father. He attempted to have Peter killed by getting his servants drop to him from a plane into the ocean, and then offered Peter a million dollars to leave Lois alone.

They married and now she is the mother of three kids, although her attitude to daughter Meg sometimes leaves a lot to be desired. She also seems oblivious to infant son Stewie's numerous attempts to kill her.

There's the possibility she had two other children as well – Peter Jr., who was shaken to death by Peter, and the 'other sister', who may have been strangled to death by Meg. The family insist this child never existed, despite Chris's memories of her.

Lois is very protective of her brood and once said: "I'm like one of those bald eagles on the Discovery Channel. Beautiful to look at, but mess with one of my chicks and I'll use my razor sharp talons to rip your eyes out."

On the surface she is the most upright of the Griffins, playing the organ in church and concerned about the running of the town and school. But this hides a rather wicked streak. She has a sadomasochistic fetish, wore bondage gear in one episode, and once asking Peter to stick his finger in a bullet hole and twist it. She even asked Brian

to kick her in the chest! Lois is the type of woman who needs to keep things buttoned down. Once her wild side is released she likes to take things to the extreme – such as becoming a crazed kleptomaniac or losing the family's car at an Indian casino.

She's also good looking with a killer body, which sometimes leads to Peter putting her down because he feels inadequate. It also sends their sex-crazed neighbour, Quagmire, into a frothing fervour and ensures Brian the dog is more than a little infatuated with her. ■

MEG GRIFFIN

"I HATE YOU ALL!"

Meg is perennially unpopular. The beanie-hat obsessed eldest child of Peter and Lois is so disliked that even her own family spend half their time ignoring or making fun of her.

Her parents even decided that if they had to leave one child behind in an emergency, she'd be the one. Peter cared so little about her that when the rest of the family went to a panic room because their house was being robbed, he sent Meg out to make him a sandwich. Luckily, the robbers thought she was too ugly to interfere with, and eventually tried to have her charged with sexual harassment.

It's not much fun being Meg. She's desperate for acceptance from the cool kids at school, especially the boys (except dorky Neil Goldman, whose unwanted attentions she's often had to spurn), but she rarely gets either.

Even when it looks like things are going right for her, everything goes bad. There was one time when she actually looked hot and ended up with her losing her virginity on national TV.

There was also an invite to a really cool party that resulted in her accidentally rolling around in a cupboard snogging her own brother! She even had to accept a pity date from the family dog because she couldn't get a date to the prom.

Meg does have a few friends, but they're the other ugly outcasts from High School. Despite wanting better mates, it's probably best she sticks with her social pariah chums, as her other attempts to make friends haven't gone so well.

Once she accidentally joined a suicide cult and then pretended to be a lesbian just to fit in with her school's Sapphic society. Luckily in the latter case, Lois brought her daughter to her senses by showing her how much better she was at kissing women than Meg.

Meg does occasionally get some affection (even if her mother did once leave her crying in her room with a bottle of Ambien and a Sylvia Plath novel, saying "Whatever happens, happens"). There have even been times when her parents have been fiercely loyal to her.

After nearly drowning his daughter by sending her to fetch a beer from the already flooded kitchen, Peter promised to be a better father if she woke up from a coma.

While he eventually decides he has to keep being horrible to her in order to keep up appearances, he tells her they can be secret friends. ∎

DID YOU KNOW?

It was suggested in the episode 'Screwed The Pooch', that Meg's biological father may not be Peter, but instead a man called Stan Thompson

CHRIS GRIFFIN

"I'M TURNING YOU INTO POO!"

A bit of a chip off the old block, Christopher Cross Griffin is rather like his father. He's pretty portly and unlikely to be joining Mensa any time soon.

In his mid-teens, Chris has to deal with many of the normal problems of puberty, from bodily changes and acne (his spots have been known to take on a life of their own) to girls and school... and having an evil monkey that used to live in his closet.

He is the dumbest but perhaps most normal of the Griffin kids. Unlike Meg, he has the ability to actually make friends. He is a little self-conscious, especially about his weight. He also has some talents, especially drawing, and once almost became a famous artist in New York where he got to date a literally two-dimensional Kate Moss.

He once passed a note to Meg saying he thinks 'Mrs. Griffin is hot' when he was being home-schooled by his mom. He's also said he thinks children come from the Child Welfare Office, and got very confused during a school project

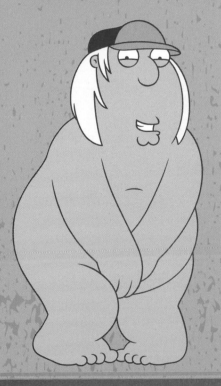

about whether a shoebox should contain a 'diorama' or 'diarrhoea'.

Much of this can be probably be blamed on Lois admitting that she smoked and drank a lot while pregnant with him, in the hope of inducing a miscarriage.

Chris also has trouble understanding love. Actually, he sometimes has difficulty understanding gender! He got very confused when his male friend, 'Sam', kissed him, not realising that she was actually a girl.

He has had a few girlfriends, including the incredibly popular Connie DiMico, his sister's enemy. He's even technically still married to a girl called Loka from a South American rainforest village, who he got hitched to when he ran away to join the Peace Corps.

But the great love in Chris's life is rather one-way, involving elderly neighbour Herbert's unrequited love for the teenage boy, which Chris has only recently realised may be something less than innocent. ∎

STEWIE GRIFFIN

"VICTORY IS MINE!"

Stewie is undoubtedly the cleverest one-year-old the world has ever seen. He is able to build incredibly advanced machines, from time travel pods and teleportation devices to a shrinking ray and a box that turns his brother Chris into a human puppet.

Many of his inventions have been the result of him wanting to keep his killer instincts sharp, as well as sometimes planning for world domination. He also used to spend a lot of time trying to find ways to kill his mother, although recently he hasn't been as obsessed with this.

Sadly for him though, others generally don't appreciate his genius and just see a baby. He has been responsible for several deaths though, including accidentally killing his babysitter's boyfriend by locking him in a car trunk and forgetting he was there.

He's not always evil though, once deciding he did love his mother, to the point that Lois felt so smothered that she hit him. Stewie's closest relationship is probably with Brian, the only member of the family who seems to understand everything he says. They enjoy a lot of verbal sparring, but underneath that they genuinely care for one another.

Stewie also adores his teddy Rupert. Sometimes their relationship seems a bit too close – such as his rather disturbing fantasies where Rupert has a

DID YOU KNOW?

Stewie once made an appearance on the live-action murder-mystery show Bones, eventually turning out to be the brain-tumour induced hallucination of Special Agent Seeley Booth (David Boreanaz).

teddy's head and a buff man's body. Stewie has a rather confused sexuality, which ranges from being sexually attracted to other toddlers, to dressing up as a grown woman and meeting strange men in restaurants. ■

BRIAN GRIFFIN

"WHOSE LEG DO YOU HAVE TO HUMP TO GET A DRY MARTINI AROUND HERE?"

As a dog, it should come as little surprise that Brian is an adopted member of the Griffin family. He came into their lives when Peter took pity on him when Brian was living as a stray.

Brian was born a long way from Rhode Island, in Austin, Texas, the son of a bitch called Biscuit and a guard dog called Coco. It wasn't a great childhood, as his mother abandoned him. When the talking dog returned home to face his issues, he discovered his mother was dead and Biscuit's owners had stuffed her and turned her into an end table.

Now he's the highly cultured dog of the Griffins. He even went to university before he became the family dog, although he failed to graduate.

Brian has literary aspirations and a yearning for love.

He adores opera and jazz, has liberal politics (although in Season 9 he briefly becomes an arch-conservative), is a staunch atheist and a member of Mensa.

Despite being convinced he should be a writer, Brian's long-gestating novel, 'Faster Than The Speed Of Love', sold hardly any copies when it was finally published.

He's shown exasperation at being unable to find a woman as cultured as himself, although he usually just goes for looks. The woman he now feels is the great love of his life – Jillian – is so dumb it's a miracle she manages to dress herself in the mornings.

Even Jillian would probably get dumped though if Brian could get his hands on Lois. His sexual attraction to the Griffin matriarch is barely under the surface. At one point they even married after Peter was presumed dead at sea. The marriage was never consummated, and on Peter's return Brian gave up his wife, feeling Peter and Lois's happiness was more important than his own.

Brian's had more than his fair share of problems with alcohol. He is also a recovered cocaine addict, after getting rather too enamoured with the substance during a brief period as a police sniffer dog. ■

FAMILY GUY

TRAVEL GUIDE

Where The Hell Is Rhode Island?

Rhode Island, where the Griffins live, may be a real US state, but it's neither a road nor an island.

Officially known as the 'State of Rhode Island and Providence Plantations', it was one of the original 13 states when the US declared independence. It was so keen to get rid of the Brits that it declared independence two months before anyone else, in May 1776.

It is the smallest of the American states. Indeed it's so tiny that the New York Metropolitan Area alone is about four times the size of the minuscule place.

Just to show what a piddly little place it is in American terms, there are 11 states that are bigger than the entire UK, while Rhode Island is smaller than the county of Worcestershire.

But it doesn't have the smallest population, ranking 43 out of 50 in terms of the number of people, with around a million people living there.

There aren't as many famous Rhode Islanders as there are for most states – hence why one of the schools in Quahog is named after the actor James Woods (who was raised but not born in the state), while another is named for Providence, Rhode Island mayor Buddy Cianci, who was popular but is largely remembered for being imprisoned for racketeering.

> ### 📌 DID YOU KNOW?
>
> Although now largely a mainland state, it's called Rhode Island because in early colonial times the name originally referred just to the largest island off the Providence coast – which is now normally called Aquidneck Island, to differentiate it from the name of the state.

FAMILY GUY TRAVEL GUIDE

Where The Hell Is Quahog?

If you're hoping to visit the Griffin's hometown of Quahog, you're out of luck, as it isn't a real place — although it is based on one.

Family Guy creator Seth MacFarlane has said the town is loosely based on Cranston, Rhode Island, a city of 80,000 people that is essentially a suburb of the state capital, Providence.

Many of the large buildings that can be seen on the skyline behind the Griffin house in Spooner Street are known Providence landmarks, including One Financial Plaza, 50 Kennedy Plaza, and the Bank of America Tower.

Quahog isn't a made up name. It's a type of edible clam, with the name borrowed from the Native American Narragansett people and language. It's an idea the town in the show takes seriously, as every year they celebrate a founding myth, which says the city was started by Miles 'Chatterbox' Musket, with the assistance of a magical talking clam.

Mayor West, who's not exactly the most competent or cleverest of politicians, has wasted money on everything from trying to work out who was stealing his water (when it was just going down the plughole), to spending all the city's cash on a gold statue of the Honey Smacks cereal mascot, Dig 'Em Frog.

He's prepared to do anything to stay in power. When he reinstalled himself as mayor after Lois briefly took over the job, he even shot someone who said there should be another election!

DID YOU KNOW?

While the town of Quahog celebrate a founding myth about a talking clam helping start the town, the community was actually set up by a British exile called Griffin Peterson. Peter Griffin is one of his reincarnations.

Where The Hell Is Spooner Street?

Located west of downtown Quahog, Rhode Island, Spooner Street is where most of the action of Family Guy takes place.

It's home to the Griffins, Swansons and Quagmire, and the elderly Herbert. It's also the previous address of Cleveland Brown and his ex-wife Loretta – until Peter accidentally killed her.

One rather strange oddity of Spooner Street is that the plot on which the Griffin house stands is not only the site of an old Indian burial ground, but for some reason was left off the map and wasn't part of the United States until recently.

This allowed Peter to set up his own country, Petoria, which existed for less than a week. The US demanded the land after Petoria annexed Joe Swanson's pool, and therefore encroached on sovereign American territory.

The Griffins live at 31 Spooner Street, the Swansons at 33 and Quagmire in number 29.

MEET The GANG

THE SWANSONS

"Bring it On!"

Joe and Bonnie Swanson, along with their daughter Susie, are the Griffins' neighbours.

Joe is disabled, having been paralysed since trying to stop a Grinch-like creature from ruining Christmas, but he's still an active cop, and able to put most people on two legs to shame.

He gets down about his predicament sometimes, but generally he's the most positive person you can imagine. He does have a few anger issues; so don't push him too far!

His wife, Bonnie, spent the first years of Family Guy pregnant. In fact she was up the duff for so long that Peter at once point demanded she either "Have the baby or not". Bonnie finally gave birth to Susie in Season 7.

This was around the same time we learned that their other son, Kevin – who Meg fell in love with in the early days of the show – had died in Iraq.

HERBERT

"Boys, boys! We can settle this like reasonable and sexy teenagers."

Stewie probably sums up Herbert best when he says: "Well, there's a paedophile up the street that nobody seems to be doing anything about, but it's mainly because he's so funny."

Yep, while having a paedo around is normally a cause for concern, in the case of Herbert nobody seems that bothered.

But it's not like Herbert can do much. Despite his attempts to lure teenage boys, he can't move without a walker and is essentially harmless.

There have been times when Herbert's unrequited passion for Chris Griffin has come in handy, such as when Herbert battled a living tree to save his beloved in the episode 'Petergeist'. There was also the time he tried to get Chris away from another old man in the episode 'German Guy' – not because Herbert viewed him as a rival, but because the other fogey was an evil Nazi!

Herbert knows a bit about Nazis. He served in the Army Air Corps during World War II, and got locked up in a concentration camp because the Germans thought he was gay. He now lives up the street from the Griffins with his ancient dog, Jesse.

Did You Know?

Mike Henry, who voices Herbert, says the inspiration for the character was a senior citizen he knew when he worked at a grocery store (although that guy wasn't a paedophile).

GLEN QUAGMIRE

"Giggity"

There is only one thing on Glen Quagmire's mind – sex, and lots of it. A complete hound, Quagmire will do anything and everything to get some tail.

He's had Asian women who he's tagged living in his basement and even invented a drink called a Roofie Colada to make his dates more, err, pliant.

Although people occasionally get annoyed with Quagmire being a bit of a sex pest – at one point the women of Spooner Street tried to have him thrown out of town – most of the time they put up with his antics, as he's a good friend.

Quagmire claims the reason he's so obsessed with sex is that he's trying to fill the hole left when his ex, TV actress Cheryl Tiegs, left him.

Having a house where virtually every surface can convert into a bed doesn't come cheap, but as an airline pilot he can afford that luxury.

Did you know?

Quagmire knew Peter before they both lived on Spooner Street, as he first met him when he was an ensign in the US Navy.

THE PEWTERSCHMIDTS

"Peter, I see you're still very, very fat"

Carter and Barbara Pewterschmidt are Lois's ridiculously rich parents.

Carter is an industrialist who owns Pewterschmidt Industries and US Steel. The stereotypical conservative billionaire, he believes money can buy you anything, including happiness, and that because he has cash everyone should just do as he says.

He has a long-standing hatred of Peter, much of which stems from snobbery over the fat man's working class roots. When Peter and Lois started dating, Carter attempted to have his future son-in-law killed, as he was so horrified about potentially having him in the family.

Although he and Peter occasionally find peace, their relationship largely consists of Carter taking pleasure in being as horrible to his son-in-law as possible.

Barbara doesn't seem to mind Peter that much. She once agreed to have sex with him when Lois said her hubby could shag any woman he wanted. It wasn't because Barbara had the hots for Peter, just that she was feeling sexually starved!

While Lois had always thought both her parents were protestants (something Peter's stepfather, Francis, hated as he was a fervent Catholic), in the episode 'Family Goy' it's revealed that Barbara is actually a Jewish holocaust survivor, whose was born Barbara Hebrewberg. Carter forced her to hide her heritage from everyone, including her daughter.

Did you know?
Seth MacFarlane uses the same voice for Carter Pewterschmidt and Dr. Hartmann (and to a certain extent Seamus), something pointed out in the episode 'Believe It or Not, Joe's Walking on Air'.

THE GOLDMANS

"Please flush the toilet twice – once for the bulk, again for the remainder. Thank you!"

Neil Goldman is the gawky teenage boy who's obsessed with Meg, despite the fact she has absolutely no interest in him.

In the third season we met his parents, the stereotypically Jewish Mort and Muriel, who look worryingly like one another.

Mort and Muriel met via a dating service, and he now runs Goldman's Pharmacy. It's no surprise he went into healthcare, as Mort is a bit of a hypochondriac, slightly obsessed with his own bodily functions. He once got so scared he thought he was having a miscarriage!

There were big changes for the Goldman family when James Woods invited Mort and Muriel to a dinner in their honour in the episode 'And Then There Were fewer'. There's no guarantee both of them will come back alive!

JILLIAN

"I was watching this TV special about this guy called Hitler; somebody should stop him!"

Jillian's main characteristic is being insanely dumb. She's still the one that got away for Brian.

After initially being embarrassed by her, and then rather taking her for granted because he felt he was so much better than her, Brian only realised what he'd lost when it was too late and he discovered she'd started dating Mayor West.

Jillian is bulimic but Brian did nothing about it, largely because he thought it made her look hot.

Jillian didn't completely leave Brian's life, and she still pops up every now and then.

Brian appeared to have completely lost his chance when Jillian married Derek Wilcox. Her canine ex gate crashed the wedding and declared his love but it was too late.

Did You Know?
Jillian is voiced by actress Drew Barrymore.

THE CHANNEL 5 ACTION NEWS TEAM

"Coming up in the next half-hour, our in-depth look at conveniently placed news reports in television shows, but first, Peter, watch out for that skateboard."

The Quahog TV news is anchored by Tom Tucker and Diane Simmons, with Joyce Kinney arriving as the new female anchor in Season 9.

There's also the monosyllabic Ollie Williams, who presents the 'Blaccu-Weather Forecast', normally by shouting short answers to questions asked of him – "It gon' rain!".

We occasionally meet figures such as Hispanic reporter Maria Jimenez and human-interest reporter Dirk Bandit. But most of the time the on-the-spot Quahog current affair news comes from Asian reporter Tricia Takanawa. She's a pretty fearless woman who is prepared to interview a mass murderer while he's escaping from jail or have potentially dangerous anonymous sex just for a news report!

Tom Tucker has a deformed son called Jake, whose head is upside-down. He also has a bit of a penchant for sleeping with hookers and loves his moustache more than any man should!

Diane Simmons also has her own talk show, called 'Diane!'. However in Season 9 we discover she has a dark side few would have ever suspected of her...

SEAMUS

"No, me father was a tree."

You'd think it would be difficult to get around when you have two wooden legs; two wooden arms and you're blind in one eye. But sea captain Seamus seems to manage!

The salty old dog is usually ready to warn Peter about all manner of dangers, as well as applying for unexpected jobs, such as the church organist and a news reporter.

His origins are shrouded in mystery. It was once suggested so much of him is wooden because his father was a tree (something backed up in the episode, 'Ocean's Three And A Half', where we see his body is wooden too, and only his head is human).

However in 'And Then There Were Fewer', it appears Seamus was once a normal person until James Woods entered his life and then everything went wrong!

BRUCE

"Oh no!"

Also known as Bruce the performance artist, he has the distinction of filling just about every job imaginable.

First seen as the clerk of a horror novelty shop, he's also taught a CPR course, been a member of the school board committee of James Woods Regional High School, is a psychic, gives out the communion wafers at church, rents shoes in a bowling alley, has been a boxing announcer and is the nominal leader of an AA meeting.

He's a busy man, who has also fantasised about everything from being a bee to a camp version of Jaws. It's also strongly suggested he's gay and in a relationship with a man called Jeffrey, who we never see.

Family Guy – Season 9
Episode

Welcome to Season 9 of Family Guy, with loads more anarchic fun from Griffin family and the other residents of Quahog.

This is where Peter gets forced into AA, Lois turns into a champion boxer, Chris becomes the breadwinner of the Griffin household, Meg gets obsessed with Joe and Stewie creates an evil clone of himself. It's all going down on Spooner Street!

Whether it's the whole town getting involved in a murder-mystery or Stewie and Brian saving Santa, Season 9 is packed with crazy shenanigans.

It seems today that all you see is violence in movies and sex on TV. But where are those good old-fashioned values, on which we used to rely? Lucky there's a family guy. Lucky there's a man who positively can do All the things that make us laugh and cry. He's...a...Fam...ily...Guy!

AND THEN THERE WERE FEWER

EXCELLENCE IN BROADCASTING

WELCOME BACK, CARTER

HALLOWEEN ON SPOONER STREET

BABY, YOU KNOCK ME OUT

BRIAN WRITES A BEST SELLER

ROAD TO THE NORTH POLE

NEW KIDNEY IN TOWN

AND I'M JOYCE KINNEY

FRIENDS OF PETER G.   GERMAN GUY   THE HAND THAT ROCKS THE WHEELCHAIR   TRADING PLACES   TIEGS FOR TWO   BROTHERS & SISTERS   THE BIG BANG THEORY   FOREIGN AFFAIRS

31

AND THEN THERE WERE FEWER

Murder and mayhem in Quahog!

It's mail time, and after World War II Army Guy gets a letter from his gal, telling him: "It's been awful lonesome since you've been away."

Peter gets a letter too, inviting him and his family to a gala dinner in their honour at Rocky Point Manor. Sweet! While nobody is sure why they're being honoured, Peter's more interested in the fact it's for the whole weekend and it's free.

Once they get to the cliff-top mansion, the Griffins discover they're not the only ones invited to the soiree, and that the likes of Jillian, Joe, Quaqmire (who brings his tubby guest, Stephanie), Herbert, Tom Tucker, Diane Simmons and Mort and Muriel Goldman have got similar invites to a dinner in their honour.

After being ushered inside by Consuela the maid, the guests gather

in the dining room for the meal (although Stewie's more concerned that he's only brought shorts, because he thought it would be a lawn party).

So who is the host and why has he invited everyone? Turns out it's James Woods, who tells them he's recently become a born-again Christian thanks

AND THEN THERE WERE FEWER — PLAY

...ING | WELCOME BACK, CARTER | HALLOWEEN ON SPOONER STREET | BABY, YOU KNOCK ME OUT | BRIAN WRITES A BEST SELLER | ROAD TO THE NORTH POLE | NEW KIDNEY IN TOWN | AND I'M JOYCE KINNEY

32

to his new girlfriend Priscilla and wishes to make amends for the bad things he's done to everybody, which range from stealing Peter's identity to blackmailing Muriel Goldman.

However when the host goes to check on dinner, Glen's date Stephanie takes his spot at the head of the table, and just as a champagne cork pops, she's shot and killed.

Stewie isn't that bothered and declares: "I can't help feeling this would be sadder if she wasn't heavy!" Everyone is convinced James Woods shot her and that he intends to kill them all. With a storm raging outside and the way home flooded, they're trapped.

Despite being convinced a Hollywood star wants to get them, the guests soon discover they're wrong. After they confront James, the lights go out and when they come back on he's been stabbed to death.

The guests quickly realise that the shot that killed Stephanie was meant for Woods too. So who is the killer? It's difficult to tell, as everyone in the house has a motive.

The most likely suspect appears to be Muriel Goldman, as Woods was blackmailing her to ensure she'd hand over Oxycontin at the family's pharmacy. The guests split up to try and find her. They have a lot of difficulty rooting out Muriel, but do discover secret passageways. When they come across their quarry she's dead too, lying on the floor with a knife in her back!

Not long after that, Jillian's husband, Derek (who Peter thinks is "A god and I will die for you

or kill others" after seeing a photo that makes it look like he's holding up the Hollywood sign), goes off to try and get a signal on his cell phone. He is hit over the head with a Golden Globe and falls off a balcony.

The survivors decide to stick together and search everyone's room, in the hope of uncovering evidence. They get a shock when they enter Tom Tucker's bedroom and find the award that killed Derek, and James Woods' girlfriend Priscilla's body hidden in a vent.

It now seems pretty certain than news anchor Tucker is the murderer. He doesn't want to go to jail and runs off with the others in hot pursuit. After chasing him around a table, the guys manage to catch him and policeman Joe puts him under arrest, adding that he's going to assure the news anchor a terrible punishment – "When the movie of this story comes out, I'm gonna make sure Adrien Brody plays you."

As everyone is packing up to go home the next morning, Lois stops to talk to Tom's anchor partner Diane Simmons. When Diane says her mom has already sent her a blouse to wear on her first solo news show, Lois realises that could only have happened if Diane knew Tom would either be dead or in jail by the time they left the mansion.

Diane confesses to Lois that she is the real killer. She only wanted James Woods dead and Tom Tucker framed for the murder, as Woods had dumped her and Tucker had her fired from the news, both of them getting rid of her because she's just turned 40.

After Stephanie accidentally got in the way of the bullet meant for Woods, things spiralled out of control. Muriel Goldman came across Diane when she was trying to hide the knife she'd used to stab Woods and paid the ultimate price. Derek had to die, as Diane couldn't risk him contacting the outside world before she'd covered her tracks.

Now she has one more track to cover – Lois – who she guides to a cliff edge. A gunshot rings out and a bullet hits Diane, causing her to fall off the cliff to her death. Lois looks around, unable to see who saved her, but calls out a thank you.

Up on a balcony, Stewie is holding a sniper rifle with its barrel smoking, and declares: "If anybody's gonna take that bitch down, it's gonna be me."

EXCELLENCE IN BROADCASTING

Brian tries out the right wing

When Lois sees that right-wing commentator Rush Limbaugh is coming to town for a book signing, she doesn't want the stridently left-wing Brian to know. She's aware that if he finds out he won't shut up about it.

But Brian's a dog and has extremely good hearing, so he knows the moment Lois opens her mouth.

Furious Brian decides: "This guy single-handedly set political discourse back a hundred years. You know what?

I'm gonna go down there and give that bastard Limbaugh a piece of my mind."

After confronting Rush, all Brian can manage to say is: "Listen, Limbaugh, my name is Brian Griffin, and I have got something to say to you. Our republic has been bastardised and royally screwed up thanks to you jackasses. You suck! And you're terrible. And... and... and you've been divorced several times."

Limbaugh asks Brian whether he's actually read anything he's written. Brian has to admit he hasn't.

BRIAN: "WELL, AFTER RUSH OPENED MY EYES, I AM SEEING THE WORLD IN A WHOLE NEW WAY NOW. TO QUOTE A FAMOUS TROUBLEMAKER, 'I HAVE A DREAM...'"

After Rush saves Brian from a beating by a 'multi-racial TV gang', the dog reluctantly agrees to give the pundit's book a try. It turns out to be a revelation, with Brian immediately reversing all his long-held left-wing, liberal values, and becoming a strident neo-conservative.

Brian goes back to thank Rush, but isn't sure how. The writer tells him: "I got the words, Brian. 'Thank you, Rush, for doing my thinking for me, 'cause I lack the ability to think critically and independently.'"

He then takes Brian off to the Republican Party headquarters, to meet the likes of George W. Bush and John McCain (who Rush knows because they used to solve Scooby Doo-style mysteries together).

Lois is less convinced about Brian's u-turn though, telling him that because the Democratic Party are now in power: "I think you just got to be in the 'out' group. Whoever's on top, whoever's in power, whoever's successful, you got to be on the other side or you don't feel like the smartest guy in the room."

Brian decides to invite Rush to dinner, but that just sets off an argument between Lois, who tries to stand up for the government,

and Limbaugh, who argues that the private sector is better. Peter doesn't know what to think, admitting: "I'm too stupid to make up my own mind."

Furious at his family's attitude, which is basically that he's been brainwashed, Brian decides to leave and stay with Rush. That doesn't turn out so well, not least because Brian decides to replace all Rush's belongings with American-made goods, which all fail almost instantly.

Rush reaches the end of his patience with Brian when the dog interrupts his radio show. Brian has become so conservative that even though Rush is known as one of the most right-wing pundits in America,

Brian thinks he's gone soft!

The super-right-wing Brian decides to step things up a notch, breaking into the office of Nancy Pelosi, the Democrat Speaker of the United States House of Representatives. This lands Brian in jail, but Rush bails him.

Limbaugh doesn't think Brian really is right-wing and tells him: "It's not a coincidence you turned your back on your democratic principles just when the Democrats became the political establishment. All you want is something to fight against."

Brian admits that deep down he is a true liberal. He and Rush reach a truce, realising they'll never genuinely agree. Even though Brian thinks Rush is a, "Boneheaded, fascist, corporate-shilling blowhard," and Rush believes Brian is "A godless, socialist, pot-smoking, maggot-infested member of the blame-America-first crowd", they realise that's just fine!

WELCOME BACK, CARTER

An affair to remember

Lois and Peter have gone to visit her extremely rich parents, Barbara and Carter Pewterschmidt. While waiting for dinner, Barbara reminisces about how she and Carter met on a balmy summer day at the Newport Country Club. Barbara had tossed a ball and spilled Carter's drink. When Carter said "Ah! You dumb bitch!" it kicked off their romance, as Barbara was so thankful that he was speaking to her.

The young lovers' romance was threatened when the Great War with Alaska broke out and Carter was drafted, nearly losing his life in battle against the infamous, walrus-riding Nanookwaffe. After writing to her every day, Carter suddenly stopped all correspondence.

AND THEN THERE WERE FEWER | EXCELLENCE IN BROADCASTING | WELCOME BACK, CARTER PLAY | BABY, YOU KNOCK ME OUT | BRIAN WRITES A BEST SELLER | ROAD TO THE NORTH POLE | NEW KIDNEY IN TOWN | AND I'M JOYCE KINNEY

36

Barbara presumed he was dead, so she took up with a young dandy named Rodginald. But Carter returned and the couple married.

When dinner is ready Peter is sent to find Carter, who's out on his yacht. Peter discovers Carter on the boat, in bed with another woman! Carter swears Peter to secrecy and threatens to ruin him if he talks.

Peter doesn't know what to do, as not telling anyone would mean lying to his wife. He talks it over with his friends Joe and Quagmire, discovering that although Glen is a sex-fiend, he's very big on the sanctity of marriage.

Quagmire admits: "Peter, once entered into, marriage is a sacred bond; an alliance blessed by God and hallowed by the community. That's why I'll never opt for the matrimonial condition. It wouldn't be fair to the historical framework of the institution. But for those who do and then turn their back on its long-standing convictions? Shame!"

However Quagmire and Joe point out that this could be an opportunity for Peter, as Lois's dad is loaded and he could blackmail him.

Peter uses the Jacuzzi at the Pewterschmidt mansion in the middle of the night (although he thinks it's a bubbly toilet), and tells

Carter that from now on he expects his father-in-law to do whatever he asks. He soon forces Carter to let him have a limo outing and a trip to France.

He also gets Carter to invent him a new catchphrase. He decides that "If you've got a problem, take it up with my butt. He's the only one that gives a crap," is the best one.

Peter screws things up as he is taking his father-in-law's big screen TV. He blabs in front of Barbara that Carter is being nice to him because he's been covering for his affair. Barbara decides to divorce her husband.

Feeling guilty, Peter decides to help Carter settle into life as a single guy. It doesn't go too well. At a nightclub

Carter reveals some rather old-fashioned attitudes to race and blows it with some young ladies. He then tells Peter: "I don't want women like that. I... I want Babs... I had a moment of weakness, but I... I know now that I was wrong. I need her, Peter. I love her. You-you got to help me get her back."

They set off to get Barbara back and discover she's taken up with Rodginald again. Peter knows how to take out the competition. He says the word 'Penis' to Rodginald, who promptly faints.

Peter then sets the mood by singing a lilting version of his beloved favourite song, and Carter opens his soul. "I kneel before you a frightened soul and a broken man. A man who has nothing without you. Give me one more chance, and I pledge to place above you nothing – not even myself – for all my time here, and for time forever. Please, I beg you," pleads Carter.

Barbara isn't certain, but agrees Carter can move back in and they can take things step-by-step.

FRIENDS OF PETER G. — GERMAN GUY — THE HAND THAT ROCKS THE WHEELCHAIR — TRADING PLACES — TIEGS FOR TWO — BROTHERS & SISTERS — THE BIG BANG THEORY — FOREIGN AFFAIRS

HALLOWEEN ON SPOONER STREET

More tricks than treats

It's Halloween in Quahog and the Griffin family is getting ready for some trick or treating.

Peter is preparing for the Halloween tradition of him, Joe and Quagmire playing pranks on one another. This year it's Glen's turn to get crapped on by the other two.

Quagmire has to put up with a lot, as Peter and Joe egg him while he's getting his mail, and then trick him into having sex with Joe by getting the policeman to pose as a beautiful woman. They also try to infect Glen

with a terrible disease, but discover he's immune to every known illness.

Peter rushes off to Africa so he can find a new sickness with which to infect Quagmire. He finds just such a disease and completes the prank, even though it causes Quagmire's face to bloat horribly and start bleeding.

Brian tells Stewie about trick or treating and agrees to take him out for sweets. Stewie goes out dressed as a vampire duck. "But I'm a modern vampire duck who hangs around with Anna Paquin and drives around in a black Mercedes."

STEWIE: "ALL RIGHT, BRIAN, WE'RE GETTING MY CANDY BACK, AND HERE'S HOW IT'S GONNA GO DOWN: FIRST, WE TRACK DOWN THOSE TEENAGE HOODLUMS AND KILL THEM ALL."

AND THEN THERE WERE FEWER | EXCELLENCE IN BROADCASTING | WELCOME BACK, CARTER | ▶ PLAY HALLOWEEN ON SPOONER STREET | BRIAN WRITES A BEST SELLER | ROAD TO THE NORTH POLE | NEW KIDNEY IN TOWN | AND I'M JOYCE KINNEY

38

Stewie isn't certain that there aren't real monsters about, and things don't go well at Mayor West's house, as he's giving out Cornish game hens and gravy. Things get worse when Stewie finds himself alone and is confronted by bullies, who take his pillowcase stuffed with treats. When Brian returns, he vows to help Stewie get his candy back.

Meg is at her first big high school Halloween party. She and her friends realise that if they all wear Halloween masks, no one will know they're the dorky, unpopular people at the school. It's a ruse that seems to work. Meg is invited to play spin the bottle and heads off into a cupboard with a boy dressed as Optimus Prime.

Unfortunately for her, when the light are turned back on in the closet she discovers that she's been kissing her brother, Chris. Both are horrified, with Meg particularly freaked out: "Oh, my God! Oh. We did so much!"

Brian's plan to retrieve Stewie's candy by trying to be reasonable with the bullies backfires when they get him alone and spray paint him pink!

Peter and Glenn go out with Joe, who's on duty as a policeman. Quagmire tells them a little of his

family history, and how his grandfather was Japanese and a kamikaze pilot in World War II. The guys think that's fascinating, until Glen comes across an old Japanese fighter plane and says he'll take his friends for a ride.

Once in the air, Quagmire starts acting strangely. "It's like something just awakened inside me. I can feel my grandfather's Japanese blood coursing through my veins," says Glen as he turns the plane and aims it at the ships in the harbour!

Peter and Joe think he's gone insane but at the last moment Glen pulls up and announces it's just a trick. He wanted to get them back for making him have sex with Joe. Turns out he doesn't even have Japanese ancestry!

After Brian's plan to threaten the bullies with a bazooka goes wrong, he and Stewie go to Plan B, which is to get Lois involved. She goes to speak to the main bully's mom and demands the candy back, plus the bully's sweets and $40!

Meg and Chris arrive back home and Brian wonders why they smell of "sweat and shame". Despite their incestuous rendezvous, Chris manages to see the bright side, saying: "Uh, well... you see, um... we, uh... you know what? I don't care. I hooked up with a chick tonight, and I am pretty darn proud of myself."

HAPPY BIRTHDAY PETER!

BABY, YOU KNOCK ME OUT

Lois in the ring

It's Peter's birthday and he's having a party – even though he doesn't want to invite his own daughter. While he's not impressed with most of the gifts, Peter does like Quagmire's present of tickets to a Foxy Boxing event, where two women beat each other up for the pleasure of the men in the audience.

The Griffins go to the fight and after watching some women pummel each other, the announcer asks whether any of the women in the audience want to take on the house champion. Lois isn't keen but Peter volunteers her anyway.

At first the housewife thinks it's just going to be a bit of fun. "We gonna pretend to hit each other for a while, then maybe kiss a little?" But when the house champ gives her a few powerful jabs, Lois decides to take no prisoners. "Okay, you little bitch, that's it! You want to (bleep) with me? Let's go!" With a few punches, Lois floors the opposition. The announcer sidles up to Peter and suggests Lois think about professional boxing, as she could make some serious money.

Lois thinks that's it for her boxing career, but the next day Peter announces:

"I'm a fight promoter now. And I got you another fight. You're boxing tonight at the Quahog Civic Center."

Lois won't change her mind about never fighting again, so Peter comes up with a plan that involves blindfolding her and telling her they're going to a fancy restaurant. Next thing Lois knows, the blindfold is off and she's pushed into a boxing ring.

Lois is still determined not to fight, but when the bell rings her opponent starts to hit her. Imagining she's punching Peter, Lois starts to hit back and soon knocks her competition down.

With the adrenalin pumping, Lois feels completely in control and loves the sensation. Soon she's training at the gym and taking her boxing seriously. She tells Brian: "When I stepped into that ring – I don't know. Something happened to me. It's like I tapped into this primal wellspring of pent-up anger that just needed to be released."

It's clear the pent-up anger is directed at her dolt of a husband, especially when he arrives in the kitchen and says he'll break one window every five seconds until he's given flapjacks.

Lois becomes an excellent fighter, knocking out the competition one

after another, until she becomes the best female boxer in Quahog. That's until she gets a broken nose, at which points she decides it's time to hang up the gloves.

However Peter wants the cash (for bourbon and anime), although even he realises that he's taken things too far when Lois admits that the main reason she fights is because: "Sometimes you're so insensitive, and you make me so angry, I just want to clock you in the jaw."

The town throws her a retirement celebration, revealing a statue of Lois to mark her 17 consecutive victories. Deirdre Jackson, a fighter so lethal that she's killed three people in the ring, interrupts proceedings. According

to Brian: "Her fists are so dangerous, she's not allowed to be a lesbian."

Deirdre thinks Lois is retiring because she's scared to take her on. Lois backs away from the battle, but when Deirdre comes onto Peter and then humiliates him, Lois accepts the bout.

Despite previously being a big fan of Lois's boxing career, this time Peter is scared that if his wife gets in the ring, Deirdre will kill her. Lois is still furious, saying: "I'll hang up the gloves after I knock her ass out. Peter, she milked your boobs, and there were a lot of people I knew there. Now, let's go."

The bout isn't the sort of easy match Lois is used to, with Deirdre blocking her punches and pinning her on the ropes. Lois thinks she has little chance. She tells Joe: "She… she's too str… she's too strong, Joe. I don't stand a chance out there." Things get more serious when they reach round six, the round in which Deirdre had predicted she'd kill Lois!

After getting knocked to the canvas, Lois decides enough is enough, gets up and starts battling back hard. After a fierce fight, with Deirdre threatening Lois's life, the Griffin mother ducks one of Deirdre's punches, then hits her opponent with an uppercut that lifts Jackson off her feet and knocks her out. Lois wins!

The next day Lois confirms her retirement.

| FRIENDS OF PETER G. | GERMAN GUY | THE HAND THAT ROCKS THE WHEELCHAIR | TRADING PLACES | TIEGS FOR TWO | BROTHERS & SISTERS | THE BIG BANG THEORY | FOREIGN AFFAIRS |

41

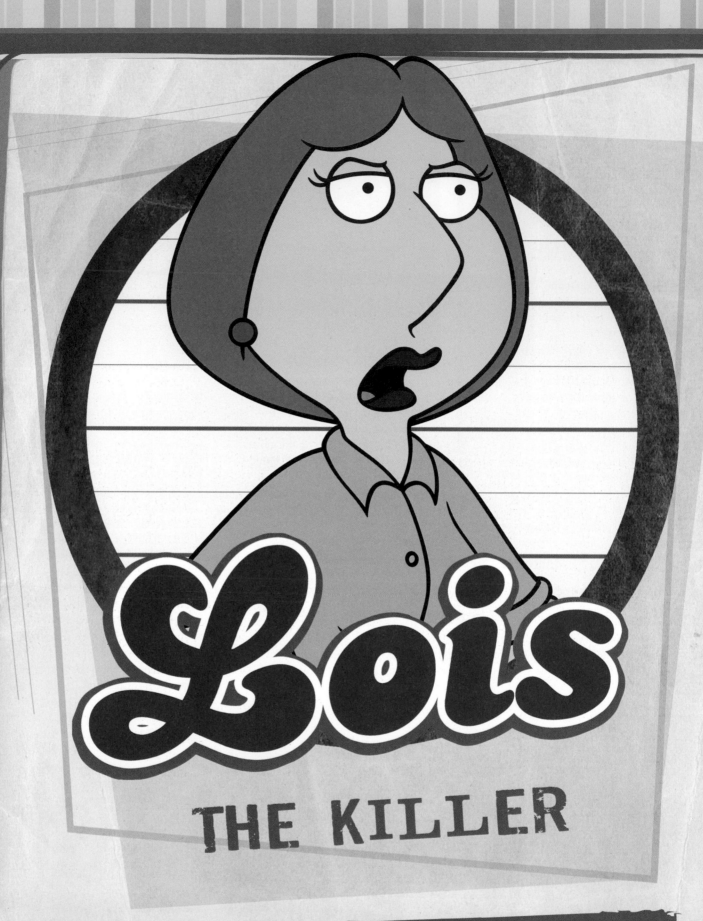

Lois
THE KILLER

WHY THE GRIFFIN MATRIARCH IS
NOT A WOMAN TO MESS WITH

When you first meet Lois Griffin, you might think she's the most prim and proper lady you can ever imagine – playing the church organ and teaching the piano – but lurking just under the surface is a wild woman just waiting to be let out. That's true of her sex life and even more so with her fists.

Lois is a woman who like a bit of S&M, dressing as a dominatrix in 'Let's Go To the Hop', and putting out a lit cigarette on her arm in 'Breaking Out Is Hard To Do'.

That episode gave us one of our earliest tastes of the woman who'd put Bonnie & Clyde to shame. After stealing a ham because she forgot to take enough money to the store, she loves the rush and becomes a crazed kleptomaniac, going on a robbing spree that has nothing to do with getting things she needs – she just want the endorphins. Lois ends up in jail.

Her true talent for fisticuffs was revealed in 'Lethal Weapons', where she takes Tae-Jitsu lessons and then

LESBIAN LOIS?

A violent streak is not the only thing hiding under the surface of Lois Griffin. Numerous times it's been suggested she isn't averse to a bit of woman-on-woman action (although she doesn't appear to want a man around when she's scratching that itch).

There have been numerous hints at her lesbian streak, such as her reply to Peter's comments that women only want to titillate, saying: "Ah, he is so right on. Women are such teases. That's why I went back to men."

Bonnie Swanson also has to caution Lois about applying suntan lotion too far down her back when she starts to get too close to Bonnie's moneymaker. The Griffin mother even snogs a teenage girl in front of her daughter, to prove that Meg can't be a lesbian if she's not as good at kissing women as her mom.

She does have a rather relaxed attitude to sex, once advising teenagers to make themselves available, as they don't know who will grow up to be famous. She also became the sex-education teacher at James Woods High and performed in a porno in her youth.

can't stop beating people up.

At first Peter thinks it's cool to get his wife to punch those who get in his way. Then it all goes too far when Lois gets drunk on the power. Even Peter realises that perhaps having a wife who beats the crap out of everyone isn't so great, after she grabs his, err, man package, and proclaims: "This is mine! This is where my babies come from!"

Things even go too far in bed, with Peter having to admit that: "Last night, Lois was the man!" Before you know it violence spreads right through the family!

Lois's talent with her fists re-emerges in the Season 10 episode, 'Baby You Knock Me Out', where Peter sets up a supposedly 'fun' boxing match for his wife. Lois decks the professional and almost becomes a professional boxer and the best female fighter in Rhode Island.

So now we know where Stewie got his homicidal urges! The poor baby never had a chance with a mother who'll beat the crap out of anyone unless she keeps herself completely buttoned down, and a father who has the impulse control of a rabbit.

BRIAN WRITES A BEST SELLER

Selling a dog's crap

Brian is despondent when his publisher returns all the copies of his book, 'Faster Than The Speed Of Love'. Despite the fact he put his heart, soul and many years into the novel, hardly anybody bought a copy.

Brian declares: "I'm done. It's over. Clearly, I am not meant to be a writer. I have tried and I have tried, and nothing has worked out. I... put my heart out there, and it keeps getting stomped on. Well, that's it, no more. I'm done writing."

He gets even more furious when he sees that top of the best-seller list is a self-help book called 'Dream Your Way to Spiritual Joy', exactly the sort of tome Brian feels is complete garbage compared to his writing. "I could crap one of

those things out in a night," he insists.

Stewie challenges him to do just that! After some initial resistance, Brian accepts and spends three hours and 27

minutes writing, "One big steamin' pile of book," called 'Wish It, Want It, Do It.'

Brian knows it's a load of pointless self-help crap, but he's convinced it's

AND THEN THERE WERE FEWER | EXCELLENCE IN BROADCASTING | WELCOME BACK, CARTER | HALLOWEEN ON SPOONER STREET | BABY, YOU KNOCK ME OUT | ▶ BRIAN WRITES A BEST SELLER PLAY  | NEW KIDNEY IN TOWN | AND I'M JOYCE KINNEY

44

what the public loves. Stewie's friend in publishing helps Brian get the book into stores.

After Stewie helps the book get good reviews in magazines, Brian hires the baby as his publicist. Brian is interviewed on the Quahog news (with Stewie being very strict about the questions that are allowed to be asked, and making outlandish demands). As Brian's book takes off, Stewie gets him publicity gigs in New York.

Things between Stewie and Brian start to go south on that trip. After complimenting Stewie on the work he's been doing, Brian reveals that he really thinks Stewie should be massaging his ego more, such as checking him into hotels and sending pretty girls to his room.

Brian's opinion of himself spins out of control. He hits on women who come to a book signing and starts to believe that he really is a genius, rather than someone who wrote some rubbish in three hours.

Brian has a blazing row with Stewie after they sit at a nice private table at the back of a restaurant and find Renee Zellweger was at the front. He screams at Stewie: "I have written a best-selling

BRIAN: "GOD, YOU KNOW, STEWIE, I-I USED TO THINK THAT JOHN LENNON WAS KIND OF A JERK FOR SAYING THE BEATLES WERE BIGGER THAN JESUS, BUT NOW, I MEAN, IT'S LIKE, I'M NOT SAYING I AM, BUT I GET IT."

phenomenon! I should be sitting in the front damn room!" Brian leaves Stewie behind on the pavement.

While Stewie realises his 'boss' has become a monster, he's still excited when Brian gets booked on the TV show 'Real Time with Bill Maher', one of the dog's favourite programmes. Things don't go well at the show, with Brian firing Stewie before the taping because they switched guests.

Brian is still convinced he's a genius, but the host and other guests start picking on him for writing a piece of junk.

After being berated and trying to defend himself, Brian admits: "I think you're totally getting the wrong impression of me. I was just trying to write something that would sell. I think it's crap, too."

His public dressing down makes Brian think again about his attitude. He goes to Stewie to apologise but keeps insulting the baby instead. Thankfully, they both decide to make peace.

ROAD TO THE NORTH POLE

Christmas is killing Santa

It's the festive season in Quahog and everyone is deciding what they want for Christmas. **Stewie heads off to the mall with Brian to see Santa, amazed that:** "Of all the malls in this great country of ours, he chooses to come here. Year-after-year. You know, I mean, who... who are we? You know? I'll tell you who we are – the lucky ones."

However the queue is exceedingly long and by the time they get to the front the rather tatty looking Santa decides to close for the day. Stewie is furious, and decides Brian must take him to the North Pole. Brian takes Stewie to a Santa amusement park, but the infant isn't fooled: "You can't jerk me around when it comes to Santa Claus, Brian!

There is a Ferris wheel here, and a guy hosing vomit! Nobody vomits at the North Pole! Except for Santa's wife because she has an eating disorder!"

It's then Brian realises Stewie wants to kill Santa! Brian tells Stewie he can't take him to the real North Pole. Stewie runs off and hitches a ride on a passing truck.

AND THEN THERE WERE FEWER   EXCELLENCE IN BROADCASTING   WELCOME BACK, CARTER   HALLOWEEN ON SPOONER STREET   BABY, YOU KNOCK ME OUT   BRIAN WRITES A BEST SELLER   ► ROAD TO THE NORTH POLE   PLAY   AND I'M JOYCE KINNEY

46

Brian jumps in his car and sets off in pursuit. When they get to Canada, Stewie accidentally fires a flare gun in the truck's cab and causes a massive crash. It destroys the truck and numerous other cars, including Brian's.

Stewie is still determined to go to the North Pole and insists they carry on even after Brian tells him that the jolly fat man isn't real.

After finding a man willing to give them his snowmobile, the duo set off across the snow on their new vehicle, travelling for hours until they run out of gas. The next day Brian and Stewie set off on foot to the North Pole.

Brian is stunned when they arrive to find that Santa's workshop is really there. But something's wrong, as it look like a horrible, smoke belching, soulless factory. Stewie remains determined to find Santa and kill him!

Kris Kringle isn't as they expected, looking gaunt and terribly ill. When Stewie says he's there to kill him, all Santa can say is: "Put me out of my misery!" He explains that he used to love Christmas but as the population grew and people became more demanding, the difficulty of producing gifts for everyone became overwhelming. "I started with one family of

magic elves," Santa explains, "and every year I needed more and more to keep up. Now they're just a sickly race of mutated genetic disasters. At least 60% of them are born blind."

Eventually the elves just wander out into the snow and die. Then the reindeer eat the bodies, which has turned the animals into wild, feral creatures with a bloodlust for elf flesh!

With Santa nearly dead, Brian and Stewie agree to take on the job of delivering all the presents and saving Christmas. With the reindeer now crazed carnivores, getting them to fly the sleigh proves nearly impossible, until Stewie puts a dead elf on the end of a fishing pole for them to chase.

Things don't get easier when they try their first delivery. Brian and Stewie crash the sleigh and then slide down the chimney and forget the presents. Stewie is concerned with Brian's lack of presentation, such as not putting the presents nicely, and eating the cookie instead of just taking a bite.

The homeowner wakes up and Stewie knocks him out with a baseball bat to stop him phoning the police. The entire family ends up taped to the floor.

As the first delivery took an hour and a half, Stewie and Brian realise there's no way they'll make all the deliveries in time - particularly as the reindeer have now decided to eat one another.

The next morning the Griffins wake up and are surprised to find no gifts under the tree. The lack of presents is all over the news. Brian suddenly appears on television, pushing a very sickly Santa in a wheelchair to show everyone what their Christmas demands have done to him.

Brian tells the TV audience: "If all of us everywhere can just cut back our demands and ask for only one Christmas present every year there may still be hope."

A year later, Santa is better, his workshop is a happy place again and the elves are busy preparing everyone's single Christmas gift. And on Christmas morning, everyone is happy with one Santa present.

FRIENDS OF PETER G. | GERMAN GUY | THE HAND THAT ROCKS THE WHEELCHAIR | TRADING PLACES | TIEGS FOR TWO | BROTHERS & SISTERS | THE BIG BANG THEORY | FOREIGN AFFAIRS

47

Road To...
FAMILY GUY

A guide to Family Guy's Road To... Episodes

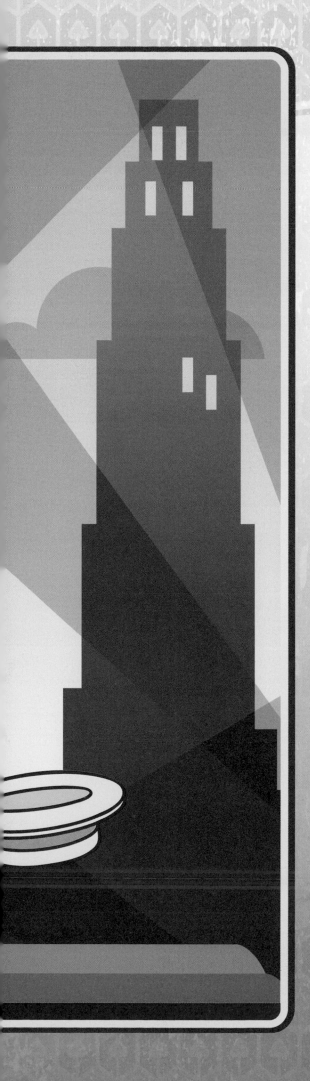

'ROAD TO RHODE ISLAND' FEATURED BRIAN AND STEWIE GOING OFF ON A TRIP. SINCE THAT EPISODE, 'ROAD TO...'' FEATURES HAVE SEEN STEWIE AND BRIAN JOURNEY AROUND THE WORLD AND EVEN TO OTHER UNIVERSES. SEASON 9 FEATURED THE SIXTH TRIP, 'ROAD TO THE NORTH POLE'. HERE ARE THE OTHERS...

Road To Rhode Island

The first 'Road To...' episode came in Season 2. Brian offers to pick up Stewie from his grandparents' summer home in Palm Springs, California. While he's supposed to fly out and straight back, a mix of Brian getting drunk at the airport bar and Stewie not realising his teddy isn't great at protecting luggage, results in their tickets getting stolen.

The duo then set off on a cross-country trip in which they steal a car and then a plane in order to try and get home. When they pass Austin, Texas, Brian realises he could visit the farm where he was born and maybe bury some of the demons he carries over his mother, Biscuit, abandoning him.

He discovers that his mother has died and her owners liked her so much they had her stuffed and turned into an end table!

Brian is determined to give his mother a decent burial. Stewie says: "I never knew Biscuit as a dog, but I did know her as a table. She was sturdy, all four legs the same length..." Brian isn't massively impressed.

Musical Number: Road To Rhode Island

Top Quote: "Oh here's a pleasant sight. Cirrhosis the wonderdog." Stewie

DID YOU KNOW?

A scene involving Osama Bin Laden singing a song to distract airport workers so he can get weapons through airport security was removed from US airings and DVDs after the September 11 attacks.

Road To The Multiverse

While at the Quahog Clam Day Fair, Stewie's ridiculously muscled pig wins a contest. He reveals to Brian that he bought the animal from a farm in the 'multiverse' that he can get to using a special remote control he's invented.

This leads the duo on a fantastical trip through multiple universes. Their first trip is to the universe where Stewie got the pig and then they travel to a dimension where there was no Christianity (and where science was therefore allowed to advance unhindered as there was no Dark Ages).

They then stumble through many universes, including a Japanese universe, a universe of nearly-naked homosexual men (which Stewie loves!), a universe where everyone has two heads, a low-resolution universe, an Ice Age universe, the real universe (where Stewie and Brian are suddenly a live-action dog and baby), and a universe inhabited only by a guy in the distance who gives out compliments.

Finally they reach a universe where humans are subservient to dogs. When Brian doesn't want to leave right away he gets in a scuffle with Stewie, breaking the remote. They make their way to the Griffin residence – which in this universe is inhabited by canine versions of Peter and his family. Stewie then realises his dog counterpart has also invented a multiverse remote, but before he can get it Human Stewie bites Dog Peter and is locked up in the pound.

Brian, Human Brian and Dog Stewie break Human Stewie out. Stewie and Brian are transported back to their own universe, with Human Brian following them as he feels he could have a far better life there, rather than being subservient to dogs. It doesn't work out too well for Human Brian who is run over by a car.

Musical Number: It's A Wonderful Day For Pie

Top Quote: "Mommy. I want to play with the new human." Dog Stewie

DID YOU KNOW?

In the Dog universe, Lois is a cocker spaniel, Chris is a sheepdog, Meg is a bulldog and Stewie is a poodle.

Road To Rupert

The Griffins hold a yard sale where Brian accidentally sells Stewie's beloved teddy Rupert.

After admitting this to Stewie, the baby does a DNA test on the dollar bill the bear was sold for and finds out who bought it. When they go to the buyer's house they discover the family has just moved to Aspen, Colorado.

The duo start to hitchhike their way across the country and hire a helicopter to get over the mountains, singing a jaunty song instead of handing over a deposit. But Brian crashes the helicopter in the mountain and they have to walk the rest of the way to Aspen.

Once in the ski resort they discover Rupert's new owners, the Cordrays, don't want to return the bear. Stewie challenges the father to a ski race, with Brian the prize for the Cordrays if they win.

Stewie believes he's got this sewn up, thanks to his incredible invention of rocket skis. The skis even grow a little house so Stewie can rest up with his butler while he zooms down the slopes. Unfortunately he doesn't realise this means he can't see where he's going and he crashes into a tree.

It appears that Mr. Cordray has won so that he can keep Rupert and gets Brian as the family's new dog.

Stewie isn't someone who plays fair and gets his butler to pour hot tea on the family's son and then carjacks a passer-by so he and Brian can drive home.

Musical Number: The Worry Song

Top Quote: "I'm buying you another Rupert. Hey, this one's cute, huh? And if we buy it, they save a real gorilla in the wild… and if we don't, they kill one. Wow, these guys are playing hardball." Brian

DID YOU KNOW?

The musical number 'The Worry Song' features Stewie dancing with a live action Gene Kelly. This is actually a scene from the 1945 movie Anchors Aweigh, although in the original Kelly was dancing with Jerry (of Tom & Jerry fame) instead of Stewie.

Road To Germany

Whilst watching the Oscars at the Griffin house, Mort Goldman desperately needs to use the bathroom. But Meg is in the main toilet, so Mort enters a pod in Stewie's room believing it's a portable loo.

However, it's not a toilet but a time machine and Mort is whisked away. Stewie and Brian realise what has happened and that Mort is now stuck in the past!

The duo jump into the time machine and discover the extremely Jewish Mort has managed to transport himself to Warsaw, Poland on September 1, 1939, the day of the Nazi invasion (although Mort thinks he might be dead, as he's managed to stumble on his deceased relatives' wedding).

The return pad is broken and the only place they can fix it is in England. With the Nazis invading, Brian and Stewie set off on a dangerous trip across enemy territory, all the while trying to hide Mort's identity.

After a chase on a motorbike and a pursuit on a hijacked U-boat they make it to England, but then realise they need more uranium fuel, which they can only get at a secret nuclear testing facility in Nazi Germany.

Joining the RAF, they participate in a dogfight in order to reach Berlin. Once there, Stewie decides to disguise himself as Hitler in order to obtain the uranium. This appears to work well until the real Hitler turns up. Fortunately they now have what they need to get the return pad working and zoom back to the present.

Arriving 30 seconds before Mort went into the machine in the first place, Stewie decides to stop the events repeating themselves by killing the Mort who went to the past with them and blowing up the time machine. The original Mort now can't travel back in time and without a toilet is forced to soil himself.

Musical Number: None – Hitler offers to spare their lives in return for a musical number, but while Brian and Stewie were keen, Mort just wanted to return to the present

Top Quote: "Hey hey hey hey! What are you doing in my room? Don't touch my stuff with your dirty, walking-on-the-street paws!" Stewie

DID YOU KNOW?

When Stewie meets Hitler he mimics him through a doorway, as if they were looking at each other in a window. This is a homage to the 1933 Marx Brothers movie Duck Soup, which features a similar scene.

Road To Europe

Stewie becomes obsessed with a British children's TV series called Jolly Farm Revue. He feels he has no prospects in Quahog and decides it would be much better if her were living with Mother Maggie on the TV show farm in London.

With Lois and Peter following KISS on tour, Stewie runs away and sneaks onto a flight that he believes will take him to England. While Brian makes it onto the plane before takeoff, it's too late to stop the flight and the duo end up touching down in Saudi Arabia! After performing a musical number as a distraction so they can steal a camel, they head off across the desert.

Things look bleak when the camel dies and the pair fear they'll have to use the animal's intestines to keep warm overnight. Luckily Brian discovers a nearby Holiday Inn. The next day they steal a hot air balloon in another attempt to get to London.

After offending the Pope in Rome, going on a train ride through Switzerland, having a bus tour in Munich and accidentally getting stoned in Amsterdam, the pair finally arrive in London.

Stewie is desperate to get to the BBC to see his TV chums. When he arrives at the studio Stewie is distraught to learn that Happy Hill isn't real and Penrose Pig is merely a Cockney man in a costume.

Worst of all, Mother Maggie refers to Stewie as a "grotty little wanker". In order to cheer Stewie up before they fly home, Brian lets the baby take a dump in one of Mother Maggie's shoes.

Musical Number: You and I are So Awfully Different

Top Quote: Brian: "Wait, wait. What are you talking about? Germany invaded Poland in 1939 and..." German Tour Guide: "We were invited! Punch was served! Check with Poland!"

DID YOU KNOW?

'Road To Europe' was originally going to be called 'European Road Show'

NEW KIDNEY IN TOWN

Too much caffeine ain't a good thing

The people of Quahog are excited as President Obama is coming to town. Chris has to write an essay about 'Hope' to mark the occasion. He has no idea what to write, so Meg gives him some inspiring thoughts, which Chris quickly copies down.

Peter is less interested in the President's visit and more intrigued by his discovery of high-caffeine drinks, which make him ridiculously hyper. He becomes obsessed with the beverages, even pouring them on his cereal instead of milk! He is so hyped up that when he goes on the gameshow, 'The Price Is Right', he spins a wheel so hard that it comes off its axle, rolls into the audience and kills people.

Meg discovers that rather than just use her ideas about hope as inspiration for his essay, Chris has copied her verbatim and handed it in as his essay. She's not pleased, especially because the principal said it was the best one in the class, and he wants Chris to read it aloud to introduce the President.

While she's very proud of Chris, Lois is less impressed with Peter's energy drink obsession and decides to throw them away.

Peter decides to make his own. Others try to stop him, with Brian pointing out: "Whoa, whoa, hang on, you're adding kerosene? Peter, that's insane. That'll destroy your body."

Peter doesn't understand how the caffeine drinks work. "Kerosene is fuel, Brian. Red Bull is fuel. Kerosene is Red Bull. Now, why don't you leave me alone while I'm doing my important work?"

The moment Peter consumes his homemade drink, he collapses on the floor and is rushed to hospital. Dr. Hartman tells the family: "I'm afraid all the toxic chemicals your husband ingested from his homemade energy drink have caused total kidney failure."

Peter desperately needs a kidney but waiting on the donor list may take months and while he waits he'll need dialysis. The only option the doctor can offer is shooting Peter in the head!

Three weeks later, Peter is struggling with the rigours of his dialysis as Chris prepares to read his essay. The teenager even tells the local news it was angels that gave him the words, rather than Meg.

Peter decides to miss one dialysis treatment so he can spend time with his friends. That turns out to be a bad idea when he turns yellow and vomits bloods.

Lois decides Peter needs a new kidney immediately. The hospital has already checked and Lois is not a match. She is a match for a sick kid, but Lois isn't that interested.

Brian volunteers to give Peter one of his kidney. Despite the fact he's a dog, the doctor seems

MEG: "YOU CAN'T JUST LEARN CREATIVE WRITING, CHRIS. IT'S GOT TO BE INSIDE YOU, LIKE MUSICAL TALENT OR ATHLETICISM OR THE ABILITY TO CHOOSE TO BE GAY."

positive. "Stranger things have happened in medicine," Dr. Hartman says. "I once tried to clone a chicken. The result wound up being a man-sized chicken that was incredibly hostile and ended up escaping from the lab."

Brian turns out to be a match. But the Doctor points out: "Well, as a dog, Brian's kidneys are smaller and don't have the capacity of a human kidney. For the procedure to work, we would need to transplant two." With no kidneys, Brian will die! The dog agrees to the

transplant, as Peter is his best friend.

When Stewie discovers the plan he kidnaps Brian, takes him to the playground and ties him to a slide. Stewie doesn't want Peter to die either though, and so eventually lets Brian to go free.

Come the big day, Dr. Hartman walks in and reveals he's found another donor – himself! He doesn't mind giving Peter a kidney because: "Well, the truth is you folks are my only remaining patients. I couldn't afford to lose two of you."

On the day of President Obama's visit, Peter is in the audience at the school, along with Brian and Lois. When it's time for Chris's speech, he invites Meg up to help him, admitting they wrote the essay together. Then it's time for Obama, who treats the audience to a musical number!

THE TALE OF THE GIANT CHICKEN

ENMITY MOST FOWL

DID YOU KNOW?

The Giant Chicken and Peter's battle nearly started decades earlier when Peter travelled to the past to the early days of his and Lois's relationship in the episode 'Meet The Quagmires'. Peter accidentally punched the Giant Chicken at a dance but a friend managed to calm the bird down, saying he'd probably never see Peter again.

Chickens are cute, right? All feathery, clucky and egg-laying. Well, not if they're over six-feet tall and a ball of barely covered fury, prepared to keep a fight going for years and never letting the grudge go! That is the life of The Giant Chicken, an enormous avian who really needs anger management classes. Peter may like songs about birds, but not when it comes to The Giant Chicken.

The feud between Peter and The Giant Chicken has been going for years, ever since the bird gave Peter a coupon that had expired.

This provoked Peter to attack the Chicken, and set off an elaborate battle that stretched across the entire downtown area of a city. The bird eventually fell from an office building and Peter landed on him.

But that wasn't the end of the Giant Chicken. Things got even more elaborate with their next battle, which took place at a train station, on a cruise ship and finally in an airport.

Once more it appeared Peter had won when the bird got caught up in a propeller – but this is one tough chicken and he survived.

The next time the duo met they battled through a sewer, subway, building site, airplane and Ferris wheel before suddenly realising they'd been fighting for so long they'd forgotten why they hated each other in the first place.

They decided to go for dinner, where Peter met the chicken's wife, Nicole.

However when the Giant Chicken and Peter couldn't decide who should pay the bill, it was back to beating

THE ORIGINS OF THE GIANT CHICKEN

So where does a giant chicken come from? After being shrouded in mystery, the probable origins of the bird are revealed in the Season 9 episode, 'New Kidney In Town'. It turns out the bird's probably the result of a bizarre experiment Dr. Hartman conducted. The doc explained: "Stranger things have happened in medicine. I once tried to clone a chicken. The result wound up being a man-sized chicken that was incredibly hostile and ended up escaping from the lab."

the crap out of each another.

Their enmity does have its uses. When Peter lost his memory, the Giant Chicken was furious when the fat man walked past his house and ignored him.

After Peter insulted his lawn, the bird hit him, which resulted in Peter's memory coming back. Every subsequent whack alternated between Peter having amnesia and knowing what was going on. Thankfully the bird had an odd number of objects with which to assault Peter.

If you ever see a giant chicken giving out coupons, just smile politely and walk on by. It's just not worth the hassle to do anything else!

AND I'M JOYCE KINNEY

Keep your friends close and Lois closer

After the events of 'And The There Were Fewer', Channel 5 needs a new female anchor, and so they hire Joyce Kinney. While out at the grocery store, Lois sees Joyce and decides to say hello, and kiss a little ass.

After saying she's a big fan, particularly because unlike the last female anchor, Joyce isn't trying to kill her, Lois is invited for a tour of the station and to watch the broadcast.

The two go for a drink later that night. At the bar they get a bit drunk and have some girly, personal conversations. After telling Lois some of her tales, Joyce is keen to hear some secrets of the Quahog housewife.

Lois admits to having an abortion, before telling Joyce: "All right, well,

when I was in college, I was in an adult film." Joyce is shocked Lois made a porno, but promises to keep it a secret. The next night the Griffins are watching

the news, with Lois keen to see her new friend. However the report isn't what Lois was expecting. Joyce announces: "It seems pornography has finally found

its way to our neighbourhood. Yes, local housewife and church organist, Lois Griffin, has revealed to this reporter that she appeared in a pornographic movie back in the early 1980s... Evidently, Lois Griffin, star citizen of Quahog, is also Lois Griffin, star of 'Quest for Fur.'"

Lois is horrified and seeks out Joyce to give her a piece of her mind. When she finds her, Lois tells Joyce how humiliated she is, to which Kinney replies: "Well, then I guess now we're even."

Lois had forgotten they went to high school together, when the Griffin mother knew her as Joyce Chevapravatdumrong.

Joyce reminds Lois of an event during Freshman year. "You told me I'd made the cheer squad, blindfolded me, and told me we were going for a special celebration breakfast. When you took the blindfold off I was standing in front of the entire school with my pants around my ankles and a hot dog in my mouth."

Joyce had harboured a long-standing grudge and was pleased she'd finally been able to get even by revealing Lois's secret.

Lois decides to talk things over with her family, explaining: "It was back in a disgusting period known as the early '80s. It was a time when women would stand topless, high on coke, on the edge of hotel balconies while the curtains were billowing around them. I think there was actually more wind back then." She didn't have any money for more cocaine after spending $399 on a videotape of ET, so when a porn producer propositioned her, Lois took the sexed-up job.

The family appear understanding but at school Meg and Chris get a lot of stick because of their mom's porny past. By Sunday Lois is keen to get to the peace and sanctity of church. But as she walks through the door the congregation glare at her and mutters, before the preacher lambasts her with: "You are no longer welcome here, Lois Griffin... Leave this house of God!"

Lois is shocked. "How am I supposed to live in this town if I'm a social pariah?" Peter doesn't know what a pariah is and asks: "What's that? Is that them little fish that eat cows?"

Brian reckons that rather than feeling bad about her porny past, Lois should just own it and not allow people to get to her. He tells her that she can only feel ashamed if she lets others make her feel that way.

Lois agrees and returns to the church. The pastor isn't pleased: "Oh, look, everybody, it's the burning bush. I thought I made it clear that you are no longer welcome here."

Lois starts talking about Mary Magdalene. "And who was she? A prostitute, which means, if they had cameras back then, I bet she would have done a porno... And if she did, I know that Jesus would have forgiven her. Am I any worse than Mary Magdalene? And more importantly, are you all better than Jesus?"

She then shows the erotic 'Quest For Fur' to the church congregation! Even the Pastor exclaims: "I know I'm a man of God... but that (bleep) is hot!"

FRIENDS OF PETER G.

Making friends with Mr. Booze

Peter and Brian are at the cinema for a double bill and rather than just watch the films Peter has snuck in some alcohol. Brian is at first surprised but decides he'll have a drink too.

The pair get steaming drunk and talk loudly. The other patrons try to get Peter to shush. "Hey, I'm not the only one talking. That big guy up there on the screen has been talking through the whole movie."

After telling the person on the screen to shut up, Peter and Brian decide to 'get him', and march up to the screen as they shout at the people in the movie. When the actors continue to ignore him, Peter punches the screen, rips it and falls through.

Joe, who's on duty as a policeman,

hauls Peter and Brian away. In court, Peter and Brian are found guilty of creating a public disturbance and destruction of private property. They're sentenced to 30 days of Alcoholics Anonymous. Peter produces his surprise witness, a puppet called Mr. Sockerby, but the sentence stands.

Brian can't believe his sentence. Lois thinks it'll be good for him, but Brian's certain he's just a social drinker, not an alcoholic. Stewie responds: "Yeah, that's like saying rappers are really poets."

Peter and Brian head off to their first sobriety meeting, and discover Bruce

is the nominal leader of the group.

Peter doesn't take the meeting seriously, and is more interested in the make of one of the alcoholic's cars than the fact he ran somebody over while driving it drunk. Brian is certain AA is completely unnecessary and that the members have: "Just traded one addiction for another. Their life goes from being all about drinking to being all about AA. The only difference is, when it's all about drinking, they're more fun."

Brian thinks he has a solution. "The issue isn't that these people are alcoholics. They just have nowhere to drink without being judged."

The next night Peter and Brian attend another meeting and take a trolley full of beer. The alcoholics are horrified. Peter tells them: "I sat here and listened to you bums the other day, and I got to tell you, I have never seen a duller bunch of pathetic

STEWIE: "I SEE YOU GOT YOUR OWN THING GOING ON THIS WEEK, BUT THERE'S A NEW TEACHER AT PRESCHOOL WHO DEACTIVATES THE CAMERA AND THEN HITS US."

bastards in my life. I don't know who you were when you were drinking, but it sure as hell's got to be better than who you are when you're sober."

Their solution is to make AA a place where everyone can drink, but away from the loved ones they've previously hurt. The group's resolve crumbles under this strange logic, and they all decide they want beer!

Soon the Community Center is filled with drunken alcoholics making a racket, and the police get a noise complaint. When Bruce sees the cops arriving, he starts to panic, but the group have already planned for this. After Peter says, "Alcoholics, transform," they quickly convert the room from a virtual speakeasy into something resembling a church, with Peter wearing a vicar's outfit.

As Joe bursts in to investigate, everyone is sitting waiting for Peter to start what appears to be a very moral and upright talk, which develops into a full-on song and dance number.

Bruce reveals he forgot to take his library book back for three and a half years because he was so drunk, and Carl the convenience store clerk reveals the reason he's so knowledgeable about movies is because he drinks a lot and barely ever leaves his couch.

Even weatherman Ollie Williams's staccato sentences are a result of too much exposure to the bottle.

It's all enough to convince Joe the noise is innocent and he leaves. Once the meeting is over and the drunken alcoholics disperse, Peter decides he's fine to drive home. But he falls asleep at the wheel.

It's seems it's all over for the Griffin dad when Death shows up. "You're dead, jackass. You died in a drunk driving accident," says Death, who then gives him another chance, as long as he understands alcohol better.

Death takes Peter to see what his life would be like if he keeps drinking heavily. When they get to the Griffin house in the

future, they see Peter has turned into an unpleasant, angry bum, who lines his family up to give them cigar burns.

Death also takes Peter to the toilet at his work, where he's having sex with his boss. Peter is horrified: "Oh, my God! I wouldn't have sex with Angela! She's disgusting!" He wishes he'd never touched alcohol in his life.

Death then decides to show him what a sober life would be like. Turns out it's not that much better! Alcohol-free Peter is much nicer but so sweet it's almost sickening. The real Peter wonders: "Who the (bleep) is this jerk?"

Peter doesn't know what to do: "If I'm a drunk, I'm a jerk, and if I'm sober, I'm a douche."

Death has the answer. "It's called moderation. You don't have to give up the booze cold turkey. You just have to be responsible with it. You members of the human race have the ability to send a man to the moon and make Justin Long a movie star. With that kind of willpower, don't you think you can learn to put the bottle down just sometimes?"

Peter promises to drink in moderation and Death takes him back to reality. At the end of the 30 days of AA meetings, Peter pulls out a six-pack of beer. Lois is furious, convinced Peter hasn't learned anything. Peter declares that he's going to be moderate: "From now on, half of every six-pack I buy is going in the trash."

PLAY · FRIENDS OF PETER G. · THE HAND THAT ROCKS THE WHEELCHAIR · TRADING PLACES · TIEGS FOR TWO · BROTHERS & SISTERS · THE BIG BANG THEORY · FOREIGN AFFAIRS

GERMAN GUY

Choosing between a paedophile and Nazi!

Chris's habit of 'personal amusement' is getting out of hand, to the point where his blanket is stiff as a board and shatters when dropped. The family decide the teenager needs a hobby to keep his hands occupied.

Peter and Chris try stamp collecting, which turns out to be boring. Peter declares: "What we're gonna do now is kill ourselves because this is horrible."

Next Peter reckons getting Chris drinking would be a good plan, forgetting that because his son isn't 21, he can't go to bars. Chris discovers a possible hobby of his own when he comes across a newly opened puppet store that is run by an old German guy called Franz Gutentag.

The two becomes friends, with Chris enjoying making puppets. Chris has so much fun with Franz that he declares: "Wow, I think you're just about my most favourite guy who's gonna die soon."

The Griffins' elderly pederast neighbour, Herbert, who's long been enamoured with Chris, discovers the teenager has been hanging out with Franz and decides to talk to Lois and Peter. His issue isn't that another old fogey is muscling in on his territory, but that "Chris is friends with a Nazi!"

Herbert is convinced Franz Gutentag is really Lieutenant Franz Schlechtnacht, the most sadistic SS guard in Hitler's concentration camps. The old man tells the tale of his World War II days, when he was a young Air Force pilot assigned as part of an escort for a bombing raid over southern Germany. When they encountered the Luftwaffe, Herbert was shot down behind enemy lines and captured.

Whilst most surviving Americans were shipped to POW camps, the Germans found pictures of young boys in Herbert's wallet, decided he was gay and threw him in a concentration camp. It was there that he first encountered Franz, who was the guard who decided

AND THEN THERE WERE FEWER   EXCELLENCE IN BROADCASTING   WELCOME BACK, CARTER   HALLOWEEN ON SPOONER STREET   BABY, YOU KNOCK ME OUT   BRIAN WRITES A BEST SELLER   ROAD TO THE NORTH POLE   NEW KIDNEY IN TOWN   AND I'M JOYCE KINNEY

60

who lived and who died.

Herbert was spared death and given hard labour but he had to sort the camp recyclables, where he suffered the terrible fate of getting sticky hands from the soda still left in the bottom of fizzy pop bottles. Peter and Lois aren't convinced, largely because Franz seems such a nice old man.

Later, Chris is heading to Franz's house when Herbert catches up with him and tries to convince the teenager to stay away from the German. Despite Herbert's protestations, Chris isn't convinced the paedophile is trying to help him and tells the old man: "Help me what? Clean your pool with my shirt off, or wash your car in jean shorts, bend over in front of you to get little bits of lint out of the rug? I know what you're about, Mr. Herbert: free labour, and I'm not into it."

Herbert says it's a choice between him and Franz. Chris chooses Franz! When Chris tells Franz what Herbert said, the old German tries to brush it under the carpet.

Peter turns up to invite Franz to dinner, in the hope of sorting out Herbert's accusations. However when Chris tries to find the bathroom, he discovers a room full of Nazi paraphernalia and realises

HERBERT: "YOU KNOW, I GOTTA SAY, CHRIS, ALL MY LIFE I WANTED TO SEE YOU LOCKED IN A BASEMENT. BUT NOW THAT IT'S HAPPENED, ALL I WANT TO DO IS GET YOU OUT!"

Franz really was Lt. Schlechtnacht!

Franz is determined that nobody discovers his secret and takes Chris and Peter hostage at gunpoint. When Peter tries to escape by knocking the gun from Franz's hand, Chris gets confused and shoots his father instead of the Nazi. Franz gets the gun back.

The next day, Lois visits Franz to ask if he knows where Peter and Chris are. The German says he has no idea, even though they're locked in the basement. The captive duo call out

to Herbert, who is walking by, and he promises to return with help.

Herbert goes home, pulls on his old army uniform and then returns, telling Franz: "I'm here for the boy." The German isn't about to give up his captives without a fight and the two decide to battle.

They're both incredibly old and very frail and at one point Franz falls asleep on top of Herbert. Later they both decide to take a break, as they need to take their pills. When they're ready to start fighting again, Franz can't get up and needs his nurse to help him.

The decrepit fight reaches the doorway where Franz loses his footing and starts to fall backward. Herbert tries to grab hold of him, but it's too late and Franz hits the floor. The fall leaves him mangled and dead. "Say good night, you Nazi bastard," says Herbert.

Chris realises that despite his rather pervy persuasions, Herbert was his real friend all along. The old man tells him: "It's okay, Chris. Sometimes the only way to really appreciate what you have is to see what life is like without it. And there's nothing I appreciate more than your friendship."

| FRIENDS OF PETER G. | ▶ PLAY GERMAN GUY | ROCKS HAIR | TRADING PLACES | TIEGS FOR TWO | BROTHERS & SISTERS | THE BIG BANG THEORY | FOREIGN AFFAIRS |

61

HERBERT

YOUR FRIENDLY NEIGHBOURHOOD PEDERAST

The first thing to point out is that Herbert is not a paedophile. Nope, he's a hebephile – someone with a sexual interest in pubescent boys. Or possibly an ephebophile – someone who likes people in their mid-to-late teens. To be honest that isn't much better, but at least we've got the terminology correct. In most cases, being sexually attracted to people under the age of 18 is a big problem.

It becomes less so when you're essentially just a wannabe paedo, who's so old and immobile he can barely groom himself, let alone anyone else. The young guys of Quahog don't have too much to panic about, even if Herbert does want to be a predatory perv. He ain't ensnaring anyone! He is very funny though, so here are the best quotes of Herbert...

"Sorry to leave you so many messages. Just lonely here. Thinkin' about the muscly-armed paperboy. Wishin' he'd come by and bring me some good news."

"HOW DO YOU FEEL ABOUT THOSE COMPUTER WEBSITES THAT PUT A BLUE SQUARE ON THE HOME OF A SEX OFFENDER?"

"YOU DON'T WANNA HURT YOURSELF DANCING, YOU BETTER STRETCH OUT THOSE CREAMY HAMSTRINGS"

"AH, YOU'RE STARTIN' TO PEE ME OFF, YOU LITTLE PIGGLY SUMBITCH."

Herbert: You know Chris, all my life, I've wanted to see you locked in a basement. But now that it's happened, all I want to do is get you out!

"Look. Everyone but Chris, keep your pants on and we'll find a way out of this."

"WHAT'S GOING ON IN MY PANTS? LOOKS LIKE WE GOT SIX MORE WEEKS OF WINTER."

"Herbert, the creepy old man who is always hassling Chris. This guy is basically a pervert, and if he looked any other way, he would not be the least bit funny. But the fact that he's so old, and so decrepit, and has a walker, and can barely move on his own, makes it funny and makes it work."

Seth MacFarlane in an interview with The AV Club

Herbert: Sellin' your old hand-me-downs?

Chris: Yep!

Herbert: You got anything that you used to wear in the summer time?

Chris: Just these old shorts.

Herbert: Sweet Jesus.

MEG: NO OFFENCE, MR. HERBERT, BUT I'M A 17-YEAR-OLD GIRL, AND I HAVE NO NEED FOR YOU.

HERBERT: WELL, NO OFFENCE TO YOU MEG, BUT YOU'RE A 17-YEAR-OLD GIRL, AND I HAVE NO NEED FOR YOU.

Herbert: Well Jesse, I guess we gotta find some other way to spend our evenings.

TV Announcer: And now back to ESPN's exclusive coverage of the Little League World Series.

Herbert: Ohhh, jackpot!

PETER: ALL RIGHT BOYS, THE BEST TARGETS ARE OLD, RICH PEOPLE. THERE'S ONE NOW. GO GET HIM.

GROUP OF BOYS SURROUND HERBERT

HERBERT: OH NO, THERE'S NO POLICE HERE TO HELP ME! I HOPE YOU DON'T FIND THE MONEY STRAPPED TO MY THIGH.

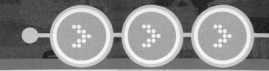

THE HAND THAT ROCKS THE WHEELCHAIR

Meg goes bunny boiler

Bonnie Swanson is going out of town but wants to make sure Joe and baby Susie are okay, and asks Lois to check on them. Lois agrees, but later lies to Meg, telling her that Bonnie wanted the teenager to go over to the Swansons' house while she's out of town.

Meg doesn't want to know but changes her mind when Lois fibs and tells her Bonnie said she was pretty. As if!

While Stewie is trying to assemble a rifle to shoot a kid at the playground, the gun backfires. Brian thinks the baby may be losing his evil edge. Stewie thinks that is preposterous, but later admits: "I

thought about what you said at the park, and I've decided you're right. I have gone soft. I've lost my sadistic streak. So, I've built a concentrated neural enhancement device, designed to boost my evil side."

When Stewie tests his device out, at first it doesn't seem to have worked, until an evil clone of Stewie emerges!

Meg heads to the Swansons' house to check on Joe and Susie. She helps Joe with his exercises, but by the time they're finished, she's missed her bus to school. Joe offers to drive her, and is even more shocked when he drops her off right in front of the school, because: "Most times people just drop me off a block away so they don't have to be seen with me."

Joe doesn't mind being seen with her, which wasn't a good thing to tell her, as on her way in to school Meg tells another student the paraplegic is her boyfriend.

Stewie's evil clone begins to cause havoc. Unaware there is another Stewie, Brian is shocked when he walks into the living room, takes the batteries out of the remote and rams them up his nose. The clone then tightens Brian's collar, causing him to choke.

When the real Stewie arrives Brian is furious, convinced it was him who just battered him. Then the clone returns and they realise what has happened. The clone attacks the real Stewie and then cuts Brian's tail off and shoves it in Stewie's mouth!

Joe's still having problems with Meg, who's now taken to wearing Bonnie's dresses. When Bonnie calls, Meg answers and discovers that Mrs. Swanson will arrive back in the morning. Meg realises she has to do something if she wants to keep her darling all to herself, and so sneaks into Joe's bedroom while he's sleeping and steals his gun.

The teenager goes to Bangor, Maine, where Bonnie has been staying, and heads for the local airport. She waits for Mrs. Swanson and drops the gun into her bag before she checks in. When Bonnie goes through security, the guards discover her concealed weapon and arrest her.

With Bonnie dealt with and Joe unaware that his wife was

supposed to have returned, Meg goes back to Quahog and continues playing house with her unsuspecting paramour. When Meg starts talking about having babies and her PMS, Joe suspects something is up. Meg then declares: "We haven't made love in two weeks."

Joe can only respond: "We haven't made love ever!" The next thing he knows, Meg is trying to breastfeed Susie!

Joe goes to see Peter and Lois to tell them about Meg's crush. Peter thinks he's just being big-headed, because while Meg did once get obsessed with Brian, that was "with a dog, not a cripple."

As soon as Joe leaves, Meg comes in to the room saying: "I can feel him. I can smell him. Mmm, I can taste him."

Lois realises Joe was right and Meg is obsessed with their neighbour.

While Lois tries to explain that they have nothing in common, Meg isn't interested, and decides to wait for Joe to drive by, before throwing herself in front of his car. Joe is shocked, but Meg believes she's made the ultimate gesture, telling him that now she's broken her limbs, "I made us the same, Joe. We're exactly alike, you and I. Now we can be together."

At the hospital, Joe explains to Meg: "I do care for you, but I care for you like I would a niece or a good friend's daughter." Meg realises she's made a fool of herself, and is glad she has Joe as a friend.

Brian and Stewie are still having problems with the evil clone, and decide to lure him out by tying Brian to a flagpole in the park. As evil Stewie prepares to shoot Brian, the real Stewie launches himself at the clone from his hiding place in a tree. The two struggle for the gun and lose their clothes, so there's no way to tell them apart.

Each of the babies tries to convince Brian they're the real one, until Brian comes up with a plan, and gets them both to look at their feet. One of the Stewies starts to laugh, and as Brian knows the real Stewie thinks his feet are hysterical, he shoots the other baby.

It appears he's got the right one, but as they leave the park Stewie turns back, his eyes glowing yellow!

FRIENDS OF PETER G. | GERMAN GUY | ▶ PLAY | THE HAND THAT ROCKS THE WHEELCHAIR | PLACES | TIEGS FOR TWO | BROTHERS & SISTERS | THE BIG BANG THEORY | FOREIGN AFFAIRS

65

"VICTORY IS MINE!"

THE EVIL PLANS OF STEWIE

It's difficult to imagine that even some of history's most evil dictators were as actively bent on world domination as Stewie when they were only one-year-old. Hitler may have done evil things in his nappy at that age, but he certainly wasn't able to create the incredible devices Stewie comes up with. Welcome to the diabolical universe of Stewart Gilligan Griffin.

Stewie is so evil that he didn't even wait to be born before plotting his nefarious schemes. He claims that before he escaped the 'uterine gulag' he left a ticking bomb in Lois womb that is set to explode when his mother hits 50 (although apparently giving birth to Chris – who was an elephant baby – screwed up her guts so bad she'll be lucky to survive that long anyway)!

Over the years Stewie has procured and invented various weapons to help him do away with Lois, ranging from crossbows and pistols to bombs and futuristic laser

guns. But he has been constantly foiled in his attempts to dispatch his mother.

His ability to invent things is truly incredible. He created time-travel pods that ended up with him, Brian and Mort Goldman in Poland on the day the Nazis invaded. He also created another pod designed to help him fast-forward through the pain of teething!

Stewie developed a shrinking ray and a ship that he miniaturised so he could go inside Peter (who he insists on calling the Fat Man) so that he could destroy his sperm. In another attempt to stop his parents conceiving a baby, he created a robot version of Peter that was so convincing, no one batted an eyelid when it insulted Lois and then fell out of the window.

The same was true when bots replaced Stewie and Brian, after the real dog and baby went off on a trip. Stewie wanted to find the person he believed may be his real father (but who was actually a future version of Stewie), and so left metal versions of himself and Brian behind to fool the family into thinking they were still at home.

Stewie doesn't limit himself to destroying Lois and trying to control his family, as ultimately he wants

world domination. Unexpected people, such as Bill Cosby, often thwart him. When Stewie realised that by going on a TV show hosted by Cosby he would have a national audience, he took along his special hypnosis mind control device, determined to make the viewers his slaves. However before he could unleash this on an unsuspecting public, the elderly comic nabbed the device, switched it on and ended up controlling Stewie.

Another of Stewie's mind control devices was more successful. In 'The Story On Page One', Stewie realised that his small size made it difficult to get the supplies he needed, so he invented a small box that he could attach to Chris's head and turn him into a pudgy teen puppet.

Chris moved around by remote control and said whatever words Stewie fed into a microphone. After sending Chris into a shop he got him to order "a hand-operated buzz saw,

capable of cutting through a human sternum. It's for a school project. I'm some sort of student sent here from... oh blast, what the devil do they study, Uh... Latin Class." Unfortunately for Stewie a homeless person confronted him and his cover was blown.

Uncharacteristically he once helped out his father, using one of his mind control devices to make a judge give the Fat Man a lesser sentence in court.

Sometimes, even Stewie's minor evil plans involve over-the-top activities. As he doesn't like broccoli, he once decided to create a device to control the world's weather so that he could destroy the plant by ensuring it can't grow any more. Stewie succeeded in creating a freezing rainstorm, but the machine was destroyed before he could complete his diabolical plan.

Other devices Stewie has created include a carbonite freeze gun, a transporter he uses to bring the cast of Star Trek: The Next Generation together, a flamethrower, rocket skis and a body switching orb. There was also cloning technology that allowed Stewie to create a new version of himself who was a bit stupider and can do hard work. Another attempt to create a clone ended up with a more evil version of Stewie... if that's possible!

Perhaps his most impressive creation was the multiverse machine that allowed the user to visit different parallel universes. There's never been any proof of multiple universes but Stewie's so smart he's confirmed the theory and also invented ways to visit them!

TRADING PLACES

Chris joins the rat race

A local Quahog car dealership is holding a 'Hands On A Hard Body' competition, where entrants must keep touching a dirt bike as long as they can. The winner is the last person with their hand on the machine – and they win the bike!

Peter is desperate to get the machine, although Lois isn't sure why. "Because this is 1978, Lois," says Peter, "and dirt bikes have never been hotter. Besides, I get one of those things, it's gonna be a buffet of beave."

Peter enters the competition and discovers his rich father-in-law, Carter, is also competing. Carter is so loaded he could buy hundreds of bikes. Peter is confused, until Carter explains that he doesn't want the bike. "But Lois told me how much you wanted it. So I decided to win it for myself just so I could destroy it in front of you."

Nine hours later, the only people left with their hands on the bike are Peter and Mayor West. After tricking the mayor into taking his hands off the machine, Peter wins! Peter gets a bit too into owning a bike, even getting a dirt bike girlfriend called Amber.

Chris is intrigued by the bike and decides to take it for a spin, despite Meg's advice not to. He crashes into a fire hydrant and wrecks the vehicle.

Peter and Lois are not happy that the bike is destroyed. Peter gets confused

AND THEN THERE WERE FEWER | EXCELLENCE IN BROADCASTING | WELCOME BACK, CARTER | HALLOWEEN ON SPOONER STREET | BABY, YOU KNOCK ME OUT | BRIAN WRITES A BEST SELLER | ROAD TO THE NORTH POLE | NEW KIDNEY IN TOWN | AND I'M JOYCE KINNEY

68

the best punishment would be to make his son smoke a whole carton of cigarettes.

When Chris protests that he doesn't smoke, Peter says: "Sure, you don't now. But keep at it. You'll get the hang of it. By the end of that pack, you'll be smoking like a real pro. Like a cool kid. There, that's it. Gettin' smoother, isn't it? Oh, yeah! Wait till you try it after a meal. Delicious! And after sex? Forget about it. It's like puttin' your penis to sleep in a feather bed."

Lois is furious and thinks the kids need a proper punishment. "You know, I don't think you kids appreciate how hard your father and I work to provide you with everything we do. Sometimes you just seem to take us for granted. You know, it's very difficult bein' a parent."

Chris thinks Lois and Peter's lives

are easy as they get to make all the rules. Lois decides it might teach them a lesson if the kids were the adults for a while and vice versa.

Soon Meg is cooking breakfast and Chris is getting ready to go to work at the brewery. Lois and Peter are convinced that within a few hours their children will appreciate what they do. But it doesn't quite work out like that.

Chris has a great day at work, thinking it's way easier than high school, and when Meg presents the dinner she serves up a gorgeous feast. Lois and Peter aren't having a great time at school, suddenly thrust back into a world of peer pressure and bullying.

By the end of the second day, the parents are ready to admit defeat. Peter tells Chris and Meg: "You were right. Being a kid is a lot harder than bein' an adult. High school sucks. Everything sucks. So let's just put things back the way they were and just

forget all about this, all right? You kids go back to school, Lois goes back to groceries, and I go back to my job."

But Chris has impressed the brewery so much that they've fired Peter and replaced him with the teenager. Lois says that as he's only 14, she won't allow him to work, but Chris is determined. "I seem to remember somebody saying the breadwinner makes the rules. Well, I'm the breadwinner. And you know what? I like being a grown-up, and I wanna stay this way," says Chris.

Chris starts to change his mind when the next day he's still at work at 8pm, and his boss tells him he can't go until he finishes all the accounts payable and the accounts receivable, which takes him until after 1am.

Peter isn't haven't much luck getting a new job and Chris is getting increasingly stressed. As big bills start mounting up, Chris's mood gets worse, until everyone lives in fear of him. Meg suggests they borrow money from Quagmire. Chris sees this as a sign that she wants him to admit to other people what a failure he is. He drags Meg round the neighbourhood, forcing her to tell people she thinks he's a screw-up. Chris grabs his chest, falls to the ground and wakes up in the hospital, where Lois explains he had a heart attack from the stress.

Peter thinks he understand the lesson of the kid-adult swap: "I guess what we all learned is that no matter who you are, or where you come from, life is a terrible thing." Lois adds: "Yeah, but if you got your family to help you get through it, it's not quite as bad." And with Chris laid up, Peter gets his job back, and everything returns to normal.

FRIENDS OF PETER G.   GERMAN GUY   THE HAND THAT ROCKS THE WHEELCHAIR   ▶ TRADING PLACES   PLAY   ...VO   BROTHERS & SISTERS   THE BIG BANG THEORY   FOREIGN AFFAIRS

69

TIEGS FOR TWO

Brian vs. Quagmire – Round Two

Peter is convinced his dry cleaner, Mr. Washee-Washee, has stolen his shirt, so he breaks into the man's house to get it back. The Chinese launderer isn't impressed and a fight ensues.

Mr. Washee-Washee wins and Peter ends up in a police cell. Brian goes to pick him up, and whilst waiting, starts talking to a woman called Denise. They discover they have a lot in common.

A few days later Brian is in love. Lois is less convinced. She's seen this before and had to pick up the pieces. The dog is convinced it's different this time.

He admits Jillian was the woman he'd waited his whole life for, but accepts he doesn't think he'll ever get her back. When he invites Denise

out on a proper date she says no!

Brian takes to the bottle. Peter thinks he has an idea to solve the problem – Quagmire's class on picking up chicks. There's a bit of a problem though, because Glen hates Brian with a passion.

Brian decides to take the class, desperate to find out how to snag the right woman. What Brian doesn't quite get is that the class is mainly about getting laid, with Quagmire telling his pupils: "You want to know how many times I've been laid since last night? 60! Why? 'Cause I'm not trying to be a girl's Prince Charming. I'm trying to be that big mistake they made at the bar last night."

Quagmire's not pleased about Brian taking the class, but the dog has paid up so he has no choice. On a field trip,

Glen forces Brian to hit on a fat chick to show what he's learned. Brian succeeds, which makes him think he's ready to try out what he's learned on Denise.

Quagmire's tips don't work for Denise. When she and Brian go out for a drink, she finds his attitude disrespectful, especially when he texts her a picture of his doggy-bits. Denise decides to cut things short and tells Brian: "You know, I came here 'cause I thought I'd made a mistake by not giving you a chance, but it's obvious you're just another typical jerk."

Brian storms into Quagmire's class screaming: "You're a son of a bitch. You're teaching us all this crap about how to get women and it's all a bunch of bull! I came here 'cause I wanted to get Denise back and instead, you ruined my life!"

Quagmire responds: "These skills aren't for women you care about, you idiot. This course is in getting laid, not finding love." He then tells Brian he'll only discover love when he finds the perfect woman – and for Glen that gal is Cheryl Tiegs.

Back in the 80s, Glen dated Cheryl for a while, but things went wrong when Quagmire got jealous of her talking to another man. Cheryl decided she's had

enough and dumped him. He's still convinced that one day he'll get her back, filling his life with meaningless sex in the meantime.

He finishes by telling Brian: "You shouldn't have tried these tricks on Denise, Brian. But if you ask me, she got lucky, because now she's dodged the bullet of being in a relationship with a loser like you."

Brian decides he's going to get one over on Glen. A few days later there's a knock on Quagmire's door, and when he answers Cheryl Tiegs is standing on his doorstep. She's just there to say hello, as Brian is waiting in the car, using all the disrespectful

tips Glen taught him to sink his paws into Quagmire's beloved.

A furious Glen decides the game is on. When Cheryl and Brian are having dinner in a fancy restaurant, Quagmire walks in with Jillian on his arm. Glen feigns that he's apologising for his behaviour and insists they all sit together. Soon the two guys are sniping at each other, telling their dates the other's flaws. Things escalate until man and dog start to fight.

Cheryl interrupts the fight: "Stop it, both of you. You obviously have no respect for either of us... Maybe you boys will get it together someday, but it looks like that's all you are...boys." With that, her and Jillian walk out.

Later, Brian and Glen are outside the restaurant, and Brian apologises: "Look, I'm sorry I did what I did. Cheryl's great, and I hope someday you get the chance to be with her." Glen admits he's no saint either, dating Jillian just to hurt Brian. The dog wonders whether it took them stealing each other's girls to finally become friends. Quagmire admits that maybe it did.

When Brian tries to get a lift off Glen, Quagmire at first motions him to get in, before reversing, hitting Brian and sending him flying through the air. Seems like maybe there's still some more healing that needs to be done!

FRIENDS OF PETER G. · GERMAN GUY · THE HAND THAT ROCKS THE WHEELCHAIR · TRADING PLACES · ▶ TIEGS FOR TWO PLAY · STERS · THE BIG BANG THEORY · FOREIGN AFFAIRS

71

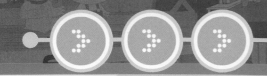

BROTHERS & SISTERS

Mayor West in love!

Lois's sister, Carol, phones up to tell the Griffins that her ninth husband, Jason, has left her. In a show of support, Lois invites Carol to stay. Peter is impressed by this and says he wishes he'd had a brother or sister like Lois, but instead got a bros-ter, who wanted to show him its peginas.

Stewie is less pleased that Carol's coming to stay, as she's going to sleep in his room, with his cot moved into his parents' room.

When Carol arrives, Quagmire's ready to hit on her. But when she tells him, "Now I know what I really need is a friend to just sit and listen to my problems", Glen decides Carol probably isn't the vulnerable woman for him.

Lois thinks she knows Carol's problem. "She has such low self-esteem

that every time a man shows her the slightest glimmer of attention, she rushes into something serious and gets her heart broken like a teenage girl."

There's reason to worry about this later when Mayor West rings the doorbell (he's ringing bells and running away, but the Griffins' is his first house and he's not very good at it yet). As soon as he sees Carol, Mayor West is smitten and Carol seems keen to go out on a date. Lois fails to talk her out of it.

Carol and Mayor West's date goes very well, with the two bonding over what seagull might taste like and why, if

PETER: "WELL, NOBODY BELIEVED WE'D MAKE IT, AND LOOK AT US NOW. I DRINK, AND YOU USE SEX AS A WEAPON. THAT SEEMS TO ME LIKE A SUCCESSFUL NEW ENGLAND MARRIAGE."

you're at the beach, going parallel to the water is the best way to go for a walk. When they get home, Mayor West announces he's had such a wonderful time that: "I want to have a million more, every night of the week for the rest of my life. Carol Yastrzemski – oh, please, let that be your last name – will you marry me?"

Lois is shocked at the quick proposal, but Carol says, "Yes!" Lois desperately tries to talk Carol out of marriage telling her: "I mean, look at your track record. Nine divorces. Do you really enjoy being Carol Pewterschmidt-Johnson-Carrington-Stone-O'Craggity-Canseco-Shteinholtz-Washington-Proudfoot-Fong?"

Peter is more excited about finally getting a brother! Lois tries to get him to take the situation seriously. Lois has a plan, having invited some of Carol's exes to drive the point home that she shouldn't be getting married again.

She shows Carol how she's called them all her soul mate or perfect man at some point, Why does she think it'll be any different this time? Finally, Carol realises maybe she has rushed things, and tells Mayor West she can't marry him after all!

The next day Carol is depressed about her break-up and has to tell her friends the wedding is off. Mayor West knocks on the door and asks Lois to say goodbye for him, saying that because of the heartbreak, he's stepping down as mayor, and heading to Alaska to become an Eskimo!

Peter is also unhappy, telling Lois: "Because you took away my brother! You ruined

my life! We were going to be brothers forever, and now he's gone!" He threatens to run away (although Lois is aware he's just acting out, because all he's gonna take is some toys and a can of tuna).

Peter points out how many people were against his and Lois's relationship, but they made it through. Lois realises that when her parents were violently opposed to her marrying Peter, it was Carol who supported her.

"God, if it wasn't for her support, I don't know that I would've had the confidence to marry you," Lois says. "And now that she needs my support, here I am abandoning her. Oh, my God. Peter, I've made a terrible mistake!"

Lois, Peter and Carol rush off to the airport, but they miss the flight to Alaska that Mayor West was on.

Peter decides to go for a drink and phones Quagmire to meet him at the Drunken Clam. Quagmire can't, as he's flying the plane to

Alaska! Lois and Peter desperately try to get him to turn the plane around, but Glen's having none of it, until Peter tells him the neighbourhood's stray cat is having kittens right at that moment, and Brian's been eyeing the litter.

That's enough for the feline-loving Quagmire, who immediately turns the plane around.

When the flight touches down, Mayor West thinks he's in Alaska, and is surprised when Carol is there waiting. They run up to each other and hug, with Carol telling him: "I don't know what I was thinking. I made nine mistakes, and I was afraid that I was going to make another one. And you know what? I almost did. I want to spend the rest of my life with you."

Soon it's the wedding day. The couple exchange their vows (with Mayor West's being the rather strange, "Milk. Butter. Cat food. Those new potato chips in the snack aisle. Beer. Deodorant. Garbage bags. Toothpaste... they're all the reasons why I'll always love you.")

The priest pronounces them man and wife, and Peter suddenly realises that while he was excited about having a brother, he also has a sister – Carol!

FRIENDS OF PETER G. | GERMAN GUY | ▶ PLAY BROTHERS & SISTERS | ...ACES | TIEGS FOR TWO | BROTHERS & SISTERS | THE BIG BANG THEORY | FOREIGN AFFAIRS

73

Love

ON SPOONER STREET

THERE ARE WEDDING BELLS IN QUAHOG WHEN LOIS'S SISTER CAROL AND MAYOR WEST FALL IN LOVE. IT'S A SPECIAL DAY IN THE EPISODE 'BROTHERS & SISTERS', EVEN IF LOIS ISN'T THAT IMPRESSED AT FIRST. HOWEVER THIS ISN'T THE ONLY MOMENT OF LOVE WE'VE SEEN IN FAMILY GUY. HERE ARE FAMILY GUY'S TOP LOVE STORIES...

Meg's Puppy Love

Brian gets more than he bargained for when he agrees to a pity date with Meg so she doesn't kill herself. After getting completely drunk and slightly stoned, Brian ends up kissing Meg and defending her honour. This causes Meg to believe they're starting a relationship, but when Brian tries to break it gently to her that it was a drunken mistake, Meg goes psycho and makes him eat her hair pie (which isn't quite as bad as it sounds).

Lois Quagmire?

In 'Meet The Quagmires', Peter goes back in time and changes the past. The repercussions of this ripple into the present, so that when Peter returns to the present day, Lois is married to Quagmire rather than him. She's desperately in love with her sex-hound hubby and his off-colour jokes, and can't understand why Peter thinks they should be together. She and Glen even have three kids, who look eerily similar to Stewie, Chris and Meg, but with Quagmire's jaw (and libido). Peter again travels back to the past and sorts things out.

A KISS BEFORE DYING

It was love confusion for Meg in 'The Kiss Seen Around The World'. She develops a crush on news anchor Tom Tucker and gets a job working for him as an intern. When she thinks she's moments from death she kisses fellow intern Neil Goldman, a teen who she normally hates. Meg is horrified when the kiss ends up on the newscast and wants to ensure Neil knows she hates him. This causes Goldman to threaten suicide and only Meg can save him.

Mrs. Quagmire

He may be a sex-hound, but Glen Quagmire almost instantly calms down when he meets Joan in 'I Take Thee, Quagmire'. Joan's a maid that Peter won for a week on a gameshow. Glen goes from super-perv to the most buttoned down, prim and proper man and decides to marry Joan soon after meeting her. Peter and his friends aren't impressed by Quagmire's change of personality and set out to turn him back. When they succeed, Glen realises what a mistake he's made but the only way out of the wedding appears to be by faking his own death.

WETTING YOURSELF FOR LOVE

In 'Brian In Love', the Griffin dog can't stop peeing on the floor. Brian goes to see a shrink to sort out why he appears to be going through a mid-life crisis. It turns out his urinary troubles are down to his unconscious and unrequited love for Lois. After Brian makes a move on his red-headed love, Stewie starts to taunt Brian with the fact he can get kisses and cuddles when the dog can't. Then Lois lets Brian down gently and they agree it's best if they remain friends.

A TRUE PEARL

After being forced to do community service, Brian is made to work with the unpleasant and crotchety Pearl, who appears determined to make his life miserable. After discovering Pearl used to be a singer whose talent was spurned, Brian changes his mind and begins to fall for her. He convinces her to leave home for the first time in decades. That turns out to be a bad idea as she gets run over and is close to death. Brian uses virtual reality to show Pearl the future they could have had together.

DAMMIT JANET

While most of the time Stewie appears a bit gay, he does have a penchant for female toddlers. He has his first brush with the fairer sex when he falls for a girl called Janet at his day care centre.
When she shows interest in another boy, Stewie attempts to make her jealous, before deciding she's a complete strumpet because she'll go with any boy who will give her a cookie.

Love Thy Mayor

Carol wasn't Mayor West's first brush with love. In 'Deep Throats' Brian discovers the middle-aged Mayor has been seeing the teenage Meg in clandestine motel meetings. Initially Brian wants to expose the relationship, especially as he thinks it will help him in his battle against City Hall corruption. However he comes to realise that the Mayor and Meg's relationship is fairly innocent, and the two just enjoy each other's company.

THE BIG BANG THEORY

Saving Da Vinci in order to save the entire universe!

After Brian taunts Stewie about buying a guy from a fashion catalogue instead of clothes, the baby is annoyed because he can't think of a good comeback. Stewie finally stutters: "Well, um, if it were you...you-you would take the magazine and you'd put it on the floor and pee on it 'cause you're a dog and you're stupid, and-and you have a weird toenail halfway up your elbow."

After wishing he had a time machine so he could do better, Stewie suddenly realises that being a genius inventor, he has a time machine!

He immediately goes back in time a few minutes so he can rush in and say to Brian: "Really? Why would I order your ex-boyfriend?"

Stewie realises this is his opportunity to always get the last word, and starts travelling back to other moments where he wishes he'd done better with comebacks – or where he can steal other people's jokes.

Brian realises what's going on, but when they fight over the time machine it malfunctions and they end up in a strange white void. Stewie decides they're outside the universe. The only way to get back is to overload the return pad and hope they get blown into the space-time continuum.

The plan works and Stewie realises that the explosion he has just caused resulted in the Big Bang, so the creation of the universe is due to him and Brian!

When Stewie heads to the farmers' market to pick up some plutonium for a new return pad, his arch-enemy and younger half-brother Bertram sees what he's up to. He realises Stewie has a time machine and decides he wants to use it.

That night, Stewie finds Bertram breaking into the time machine. The ginger youngster tells him: "You don't realise it yet, but your life is about to cease to exist. I am going to kill one

of your ancestors, effectively erasing you from history!"

Bertram disappears into the past, and soon afterwards strange waves of light appear all over the house. The cosmos is breaking down, because if Bertram goes back and stops Stewie's birth the baby can't cause the Big Bang and there will be no universe! The light is creation fading out of existence!

Stewie and Brian jump into the time machine, desperate to stop Bertram. They follow him to a Renaissance-era Italian workshop, arriving there a few minutes before their nemesis.

But this isn't just any workshop – they're in the studio of Leonardo Da Vinci. The painter of the Mona Lisa is Stewie's ancestor that Bertram wants to kill! As Stewie's half-brother, he needs to ensure he snuffs out Stewie's genius without affecting his own.

Bertram tries to kill Da Vinci by throwing a knife at him, but Stewie manages to block the knife. The two toddlers engage in an epic battle, with the duo stealing Leonardo's famous glider and helicopter and chasing each other through the street and canals of Venice.

Stewie thinks he's won when he explodes Bertram's glider

with a rocket and it crashes to the ground. However, as Da Vinci and Stewie arrive at the wreckage, Bertram leaps out holding a crossbow.

Stewie tries to explain that killing Da Vinci won't just be the end of him but of the whole universe. However, his half brother is so keen on ridding himself of his enemy that he decides that the end of everything is worth it!

Bertram shoots Leonardo with the crossbow and the painter falls to the ground. Bertram then attacks Stewie with a rock. Stewie manages to grab the crossbow and shoots his half-brother in the head, killing him!

It's too late for Da Vinci though, who's also dead. Stewie wonders why

the universe hasn't ended. The only solution is that the littlest Griffin will still be born. The only way for that to happen is for Stewie to take Da Vinci's place and leave behind his own genetic information. This will then be passed down through the generations, ready for his birth. Stewie will have to stay in the Renaissance period to keep the universe intact.

Brian heads back to the present alone, thinking that he'll never see Stewie again. Back home, a priest arrives with a letter for Brian that the Vatican has held onto for 500 years. The note tells the dog that, in the past, Stewie was planning to build a cryogenic stasis device so that he can stay in suspended animation for the next half a millennium, and that the machine should have been buried exactly where the Griffins' house now stands.

The dog rushes to the basement and starts digging, eventually uncovering the device holding Stewie. Stewie tells Brian that shortly after the canine left him in the past, he managed to 'inject' his DNA into Da Vinci's girlfriend. Brian says that means he must had sex with somebody, but Stewie is adamant, saying: "No, what are you not getting? I put a sample of my DNA in a syringe and I injected her on the staircase, the couch and the balcony."

Whatever happened between the baby and Leonardo's girlfriend, it worked, and the universe can keep on going.

FRIENDS OF PETER G. | GERMAN GUY | THE HAND THAT ROCKS THE WHEELCHAIR | TRADING PLACES | TIEGS FOR TWO | BROTHERS & SISTERS | ▶ PLAY THE BIG BANG THEORY

77

FOREIGN AFFAIRS

Bonnie wants to try out more than just the baguettes in France

Lois is off on holiday to Paris with Bonnie – whose wheelchair-bound husband can't go because: "Joe hates to fly 'cause they always put him underneath with the dogs."

Peter is already annoyed that he might have to hear boring stories about holidays when she returns.

His wife is barely out of the house when Peter throws out the lists and plans she's left for him. He sees a reports on the news suggesting it's possible people might catch goat flu, and so he decides to take Meg and Chris out of school and teach them himself.

In Paris, Lois is keen to get out of the hotel and see the sights. She's fascinated by the different cultures, and says: "Not a lot of people of colour here, but the ones that are black are really black."

Bonnie has other ideas: "Uh, Lois, I should probably tell you I didn't come all the way here to go to museums and shops... I came here to have an affair!"

Back in Quahog, Peter the teacher has his own ideas about how people should learn. Sadly this doesn't involve study and books – but taking his tie off (although he seems to think teachers normally wear tuxedos and Dracula capes), then stripping naked and racing around the room on a little foot scooter.

Chris follows his father's example, shouting: "Yay, learning!" and gets an A. Meg is unimpressed and earns an F.

Lois hopes Bonnie will forget about her plan to have an affair, but Joe's wife is determined. Bonnie checks out all the guys that pass them by in Paris. Lois says: "I just can't believe you'd throw away all those years with Joe just to have some silly fling."

Bonnie replies: "I'm not throwing anything away. Joe and I have been growing apart for a long time. Besides, we've had a good run. We've been married for 80 years." Lois is slightly confused by the number, but Bonnie explains: "That's in married-to-a-handicapped-guy years."

A French man sidles up to the American ladies with the Gallic chat-up line: "Would you like to sample a warm French baguette?" Lois berates her friend and tries to convince Bonnie that while no marriage is perfect, she gave herself to Joe and they have a daughter together. Bonnie feels she and Joe have drifted apart but she appears to be coming round to Lois' way of thinking.

Peter is still trying to teach, telling his kids such important 'facts' as how everyone during pioneer days was constantly preparing for their imminent death; Henry VIII might have kept his beheaded

wives' heads for sexual purposes; Joseph Smith only said he'd found the Book Of Mormon so people would sleep with him; and that 1985 was important for bringing us the "gayest music video of all time" – Mick Jagger and David Bowie's Dancing In The Streets.

Although Lois thinks she's talked Bonnie out of having an affair, she gets a shock when she arrives back at the hotel to find that her married friend has male company. It turns out Bonnie might have a bit of a fetish for disabled people, as the French guy she's with is also in a wheelchair.

In Quahog, even Chris is confused by his father's teaching style.

He asks: "Why is every day an introduction to the course?" Peter replies: "Now I know some teachers think they're working outside the box when they have class on the lawn. Well, I'm gonna take it a step further. We're gonna do peyote in the desert."

Bonnie is ever more enamoured with her new beau, Francois. After a few days, he asks her to stay with

him in Paris. Bonnie appears tempted. Annoyed with Lois' meddling, Bonnie tells her: "I invited you on this trip to hang out while I have sex with strangers, and this is how you repay me?"

Meg is fed up with home schooling and tries to convince Peter that, with the goat flu threat over, they should go back to school. Peter thinks he's doing great and that his daughter just doesn't appreciate how much she's learned. When he tries to prove his point by firing questions at Chris, he realises his son doesn't know anything and his kids do need to go back to school.

It's nearly time for Lois and Bonnie to return to Rhode Island, but Bonnie announces she's going to stay in Paris with Francois. Lois has prepared for this and has flown over Joe, to convince his wife to come back to him. Francois is there too, ready to try and keep his new lady.

Joe tells Bonnie: "I didn't think it would have to come to this, but I can see there's only one way left to prove my love to you." The paralysed Joe pushes himself up from his wheelchair and takes a few steps towards his wife. It seems like a miracle and Bonnie is stunned. She decides that Joe really is the man for her and promises to go home with him.

What she couldn't see was that Quagmire is secretly taped to Joe's back, allowing him to walk.

WHO ELSE BUT QUAGMIRE?

"GIGGITY-GIGGITY-GIGGITY-GIGGITY, LET'S HAVE SEX!"

"WHOA, TRANSVESTITE! BACK OFF! WAIT A SEC, PRE-OP OR POST-OP?"

FROM: LETHAL WEAPONS

Quite how he's not on a sex offender's register is anyone's guess, but most of the time nobody in Spooner Street appears too bothered about having a man like Quagmire living next to them.

It's slightly odd, as he's the type of guy who isn't horrified because he wakes up and there's a giraffe sticking its head through his window – just that it's a different giraffe from the night before.

He's a man who opens the door dressed as a baby, and then tries to convince his friends that he's hosting a family game night, but the only game he can think to tell them he's playing is sex!

There's little doubt that he's very successful with the ladies (and

QUAGMIRE VS. BRIAN

In the early days of Family Guy, Quagmire and Brian appeared to get on okay, but then they grew apart. Brian had no idea how much they had drifted away from each other until the episode 'Jerome Is The New Black'. Determined to get Quagmire to like him, Brian's plans fell apart and he got more than he bargained for when Quagmire launched into a rant about exactly why he hated the dog. So exactly what's Glen's problem with Brian?

"You are the worst person I know. You constantly hit on your best friend's wife. The man pays for your food and rescued you from certain death, and this is how you repay him? And to add insult to injury you defecate all over his yard. And you're such a sponge. You pay for nothing. You always say, 'Oh, I'll get you later' but 'later' never comes. And what really bothers me is you pretend you're this deep guy who loves women for their souls when all you do is date bimbos. Yeah, I date women for their bodies but at least I'm honest about it. I don't buy them a copy of Catcher in the Rye and then lecture them with some seventh grade interpretation of how Holden Caulfield is some profound intellectual. He wasn't! He was a spoiled brat! And that's why you like him so much – he's you! God, you're pretentious! And you delude yourself by thinking you're some great writer, even though you're terrible! You know, I should have known Cheryl Tiegs didn't write me that note. She would have known there's no 'a' in the word 'definite'. And I think what I hate most about you is your textbook liberal agenda, how we should 'legalise pot, man,' how big business is crushing the underclass, how homelessness is the biggest tragedy in America. Well, what have you done to help? I work down at the soup kitchen, Brian. Never seen you down there! You wanna help? Grab a ladle! And by the way, driving a Prius doesn't make you Jesus Christ! Oh, wait! You don't believe in Jesus Christ or any religion for that matter, because religion is for idiots! Well, who the hell are you to talk down to anyone? You failed college twice, which isn't nearly as bad as your failure as a father! How's that son of yours you never see? But you know what? I could forgive all of that, all of it, if you weren't such a bore! That's the worst of it, Brian. You're just a big, sad, alcoholic bore. Well, see ya, Brian! Thanks for the steak!"

"WE KNOW YOU HAVE YOUR CHOICE IN AIRPORT SEX, AND WE THANK YOU FOR CHOOSING QUAGMIRE. PLEASE EXERCISE CAUTION WHEN STANDING UP, AS THE CONTENTS IN YOUR PANTIES MAY HAVE SHIFTED DURING COITUS."

FROM: AIRPORT '07

sometimes inadvertently the men), even if he does look a little like he's just fallen out of the 1950s.

It's a miracle women fall for his charms with chat up lines such as: "If I could rearrange the alphabet, I would put 'U' and 'I' together", and "You must be a parking ticket, 'cos you got fine written all over you."

He will do absolutely anything get a woman to 'Gigoogity his geshmoingen', from offering them a coat with one of the arms stitched to his groin, to spiking a lady's drink so he can have his wicked way with her!

There's virtually nothing he hasn't done, whether it's trying to set up a three-way that includes his mother, or even reciting the Pledge Of Allegiance while giving a spider monkey a reach around.

It's probably best to avoid him (unless you're a complete nympho, of course), but there's little doubt he's very funny and often a very loyal friend.

THE ULTIMATE Family Guy QUIZ

PART 1

1. In what year did the first episode of Family Guy air?

2. What was the name of the first episode?

3. Bonnie Swanson was pregnant for the first few seasons. In which season did she finally give birth?

4. What is the name of Herbert's dog?

5. The Swansons didn't arrive on Spooner Street until the fifth episode. What happened to the Griffins' previous neighbour?

6. When Chris almost became a famed New York artist, what name was he given by his backer?

7. What was the name of Lois's aunt, who Peter used to work for as a towel boy?

8. In the episode 'Da Boom', Peter correctly predicts the end of the world on January 1, 2000. Afterwards, why does he insist his family go to Natick, Massachusetts?

9. In the episode 'The King Is Dead', Lois takes over as Musical Director of the Quahog Players' theatre group. What musical production does she decide to stage?

10. In 'If I'm Dying, I'm Lying', which fictional TV show does Peter manage to save from cancellation by pretending Chris is dying?

11. Although Ollie Williams usually presents the Channel 5 Weather, what was unusual about another weather presenter called Greg?

12. In 'Fifteen Minutes Of Shame', what was the name of the reality show featuring the Griffins?

Do you think you know everything there is to know about Family Guy? Reckon there's no joke, character or reference you're not aware of? Now it's time to prove it with the Ultimate Family Guy Quiz. Split into five parts, there are 125 questions ranging from the easy to the fiendishly difficult. Have a go at all the questions, check the answers on page 140 and then add up your score and find out if you're a Family Guy dunce or the most Quahog-literate person on the planet.

13. And when the Griffins ended up getting fired from their own reality show, which US TV stars were hired to replace Peter and Lois?

14. The same episode also featured the very first appearance of which recurring character?

15. What was the name of Brian's mother?

16. Brian has a rarely mentioned son. What's his name?

17. In 'He's Too Sexy For His Fat', which club is Peter invited to join after having liposuction and plastic surgery?

18. When the Griffin house becomes an independent nation in 'E. Peterbus Unum', what does Peter call his new country?

19. Meg was the President of the Quahog chapter of which 1990s TV star's fan club, as revealed in 'The Story On Page One'?

20. What is the name of the flamboyant owner of the Pawtucket Patriot Brewery?

21. In 'The Thin White Line', Brian gets a job with the police, but what ends his law enforcement career?

22. Brian accidentally ends up directing what sort of films in 'Brian Does Hollywood'?

23. What is the name of the cigarette company that buys the toy factory where Peter works in the early seasons of Family Guy?

24. What's the name of the British man who buys the Clam's Head pub and then burns it down for the insurance money in 'One If By Clam, Two If By Sea'?

25. In 'Death Lives', what musician does Peter get to play for Lois on a golf course, in order to save their marriage?

TURN TO PAGE 140 FOR THE ANSWERS

SEASON 1 & 2

HIGHTLIGHTS

HIGHLIGHT 5 HIGHLIGHT — Peter, Peter, Caviar Eater

Peter is gutted when he learns Lois's Aunt Marguerite is coming to stay, but things perk up when she drops dead on the doorstep and the Griffins learn they've inherited her palatial summer home, Cherrywood Manor.

However, Peter finds it difficult to fit in with the bluebloods, having a knack for saying completely inappropriate things that shock his posh new neighbours.

Brian tries to teach Peter to be a gentleman, but his shock therapy tactics go a little too far and Peter ends up believing he's an ultra-rich snoot, bidding $100 million for a vase, despite having little cash.

After being snapped out of his delusion, Peter must find a way to come up with the money, but even selling the house won't cover the debt.

TOP MOMENT: THE MUSICAL NUMBER, 'THIS HOUSE IS FREAKIN' SWEET'

TOP QUOTE: "IF I EVER GO BACK TO QUAHOG, IT'LL BE JUST SO THAT I CAN POKE POOR PEOPLE WITH A STICK!" CHRIS

HIGHLIGHT 4 HIGHLIGHT — Da Boom

It's the eve of the new Millennium, and a man in a chicken costume warns Peter that because of the Y2K bug, the end of the world is coming!

The gullible Griffin believes what he hears, and even though his family think he's being foolish, he forces them to wait out the apocalypse in the basement rather than go partying.

But it turns out Peter is right! All of America's nuclear weapons launch moments after midnight. When food starts running out, Peter insists they find the Twinkee Factory in Natick, Massachusetts, as Twinkees are the only food that can survive a nuclear holocaust.

Once there, Peter decides to set up a new town, with him in charge – New Quahog.

TOP MOMENT: PETER'S LENGTHY BATTLE WITH THE GIANT CHICKEN, WHICH IS THE FIRST TIME WE MEET THE CHARACTER

TOP QUOTE: "OH, DEAR ME, YES, YES. THIS IS HOW I WANTED TO ENTER THE NEW MILLENNIUM. LOCKED IN A BASEMENT WITH IMBECILES DRESSED LIKE A GAY NEIL ARMSTRONG." STEWIE

Death Is A Bitch

Peter discovers the grave repercussions of trying to get out of paying a medical bill, when Death turns up on the doorstep insisting Peter must be deceased as it says so on his hospital form.

Peter isn't that keen on dying and tries to outrun Death's clammy fingers. When Death falls over and sprains his ankle Lois realises this may be the break they need.

If they can keep Death at bay by allowing him to rest up on the sofa while his ankle heals, the family can keep Peter alive. The only problem is that with Death debilitated, no one in the world can die, a fact the Grim Reaper is determined to keep secret.

But Peter lets lots of people know that the rules of death no longer apply. Death then insists Peter put things right, by becoming the Grim Reaper!

TOP MOMENT: AFTER DARING ASIAN REPORTER TRICIA TAKANAWA TO SHOOT HIM IN THE HEAD, PETER PRETENDS SHE'S SERIOUSLY INJURED HIM, BEFORE REVEALING IT DIDN'T HURT AT ALL.

TOP QUOTE: "COULD YOU REPEAT THAT, PLEASE, PETER? I BELIEVE I HAD SOMETHING CRAZY IN MY EAR." CLEVELAND

If I'm Dying' I'm Lyin'

Peter is gutted when NBC cancels his and Chris's favourite TV show, 'Gumbel 2 Gumbel Beach Justice'.

He becomes determined to do everything in his power to get it back on the air. Peter hatches a plan that involves pretending Chris is dying so the 'Grant-A-Dream Foundation' will agree to the teenagers' wish to get the series back on TV.

However the 'Grant-A-Dream Foundation' and NBC want the rights to Chris's death in return for the wish. Things get more out of hand when a group of people turn up on the lawn to hold a vigil for the supposedly dying Chris.

With NBC getting suspicious about Chris's seemingly rude health, Peter announces to the world he's healed his son! Surprisingly, people take Peter's claim at face value, and he is hailed as the great healer of Quahog, with a cult following.

This doesn't please God who starts sending plagues against the Griffins.

TOP MOMENT: GOD TRYING TO BREAK IN A NEW SECRETARY, WHO SEEMS TO THINK HE'S CALLED MR. PATTERSON

TOP QUOTE: "HEY, LOIS, GIVE CHRIS A BREAK. I MEAN, NO TV? SO, HE FAILED A CLASS. IT'S NOT LIKE HE FELT UP HIS COUSIN IN THE GARAGE THAT THANKSGIVING WHEN I WAS 19." PETER

E. PETERBUS UNUM

Peter wants to build a pool in his backyard, but when he goes to Mayor West to get a permit discovers his property missing from the map and that it isn't part of the United States!

This allows Peter to set up his own tiny, four-bedroom republic – Petoria – with himself as the President.

Peter soon starts abusing his position, and whenever he goes into the US declares diplomatic immunity so he can't be arrested for any crimes. He also gets annoyed at the UN, as nobody seems to care about his miniature country.

Then the delegate from Iraq tells him that if he wants to be taken seriously he has to invade somewhere! Peter decides to annexe the Swanson's backyard, declaring it to be Joehio. The US isn't impressed and Griffins find themselves surrounded by tanks.

TOP MOMENT: PETER HOLDING A BACKYARD BARBEQUE FOR HIS NEW FRIENDS – INCLUDING IRAQ, IRAN AND AFGHANISTAN!

TOP QUOTE: "I WAS GONNA CALL IT PETERLAND, BUT THAT GAY BAR AT THE AIRPORT ALREADY TOOK IT." PETER

WHAT'S THE WORD?

THE BEST QUOTES OF PETER GRIFFIN

"JEWS ARE GROSS, LOIS. IT'S THE ONLY RELIGION WITH THE WORD 'EW' IN IT."

From: Family Goy

"Lois, this family believes in the Easter bunny. He died for our sins in that helicopter crash."

From: Family Goy

"I'm not being insensitive, Lois. I just don't see why we have to cancel our vacation, just because the dog's a coke-fiend."

From: The Thin White Line

Lois: Before you sit down, we're due at Joe and Bonnie's for egg nog.

Peter: Lois, can't we tell them that your mother died?

Lois: Peter, I'm not going to lie about something like that.

Peter: All right, all right, I'll kill your mother. God, when did Christmas become so complicated?

From: A Very Special Family Guy Freakin' Christmas

Cleveland: Guns only lead to trouble.

Peter: That's right. And when trouble comes, we'll be ready to blow its freakin' head off.

From: Da Boom

PETER: What the hell was that?

DR. HARTMAN: Mr. Griffin, that was a prostate exam.

PETER: Shut up! You had your finger in my ass!

From: Stewie Loves Lois

"I'm abstinent, Lois. It's all in these pamphlets Meg brought home from school. Sex turns straight people gay and turns gays into Mexicans. Everyone goes down a notch."

From: Prick Up Your Ears

PETER: (to his therapist) Every time my daughter opens her mouth, I just wanna punch her in the face, she's really annoying.

From: Saving Private Brian

LOIS: Wait a minute, where's Meg?

BRIAN: I don't know.

STEWIE: I didn't see her.

CHRIS: Yeah, I kinda thought you guys would attend to that.

LOIS: Peter, you got to go back and get her!

PETER: Oh, yeah, right, like I'm going back for Meg.

LOIS: Peter!

PETER: Lois, damn it, we both agreed, remember? If we could only save two, we leave Meg.

From: Petergeist

JOE: Hey Peter, what's up?

PETER: Joe, I just, umm, just recently found out that I'm, umm, I'm mentally retarded, and I just wanted to ask, umm, how do you deal with it?

JOE: Peter, I'm handicapped, not retarded.

PETER: Okay, now we're splitting hairs.

From: Petarded

"Lois, before I found these movies, women only made me cry through my penis. Now they make me cry through my eyes."

From: Chick Cancer

(On first seeing Joe) "Holy crip, he's a crapple."

From: A Hero Sits Next Door

"You know, I always thought that dogs, uh, laid eggs. And today, I learned something."

From: Screwed The Pooch

"I HAD SUCH A CRUSH ON HER… UNTIL I MET YOU, LOIS. YOU'RE MY SILVER MEDAL."

From: Let's Go To The Hop

LOIS: I'm not getting my tubes tied. You should get a vasectomy.

PETER: First of all, I don't know what that is. And second, no freakin' way!

From: Sibling Rivalry

"YOU WANNA TALK ABOUT AWKWARD MOMENTS? ONCE, DURING SEX, I CALLED LOIS 'FRANK'. YOUR MOVE, SHERLOCK."

From: One If By Clam, Two If By Sea

"Well, I got the idea to build a panic room after I saw that movie The Butterfly Effect. I thought, 'Wow, this is terrible. I wish I could escape to a place where this movie couldn't find me.'"

From: Untitled Family Guy History

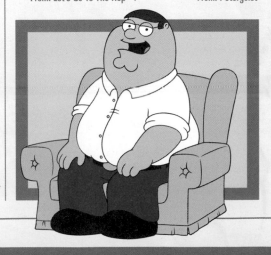

FAMILY GUY CROSSWORD

ACROSS

1. US state in which Family Guy is set (5,6)
3. Civic leader of Quahog (5,4)
5. Brian's rather dumb ex-girlfriend
6. Lois' homicidal brother
11. Stewie's favourite teddy bear
15. Surname of Mort and Muriel
16. Has been voiced by both Lacey Chabert and Mila Kunis (3,7)
17. Country in which Peter was born
19. Sex-obsessed Griffin neighbour (4,8)
20. First name of Peter's deeply religious step-father
21. Mort's son, who has a crush on Meg
23. Joe's baby daughter
25. Joe's son, who died in Iraq
26. Brian's gay cousin
28. Lois' maiden name
30. Musical instrument that Lois gives lessons in
31. Lois' sister
33. The town where the Griffins reside
34. Name of Stewie's mentally subnormal clone (5,5)
36. African-American former neighbour of the Griffins (9,5)
37. Stewie's half-brother, born due to an accident at a sperm bank
38. Name of Herbert's dog
39. The brewery Peter works for (also his favourite beer) (9,7)

DOWN

2. Host of Channel 5's Blaccu Weather Forecast (5,8)
4. Peter's mother's first name
7. First name of Meg's bitchy but beautiful enemy at school
8. Stewie's middle name
9. Patriarch of the Family Guy clan (5,7)
10. Male anchor of the Channel 5 news (3,6)
12. Actor who voices Joe Swanson (7,9)
13. Spooner Street's friendly neighbourhood pedophile
14. Peter's dead pet goldfish (11,5,5)
18. Name of Peter's biological father (6,10)
22. First name of Joe's wife
24. New female anchor of Channel 5 news, introduced in Season 9 (5,6)
27. Main Family Guy character voiced by Seth Green (5,7)
29. Street on which the Griffins live (7,5)
31. TV actress Quagmire claims is the love of his life (6,5)
32. Forename of Peter's father-in-law
35. Furniture polish obsessed Mexican maid

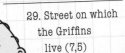

88

TEST YOUR KNOWLEDGE OF FAMILY GUY, ITS CHARACTERS AND LOCATIONS WITH THIS CROSSWORD. DO YOU HAVE WHAT IT TAKES TO GET ALL THE CLUES AND FILL IN THE GRID?

SAY HELLO TO

Death!

"I'M CALISTA FLOCKHART.
WHO DO YOU THINK I AM? I'M DEATH."

The world of Family Guy isn't quite like the normal world. After all, it's unlikely any of us has to worry that the knock at the door will literally be Death. But you do on Spooner Street.

The Griffins first came up against the robed reaper in 'Death Is A Bitch', when Peter said he was deceased on his hospital form, with Death turning up to collect the body. Peter got away with it that time, thanks to Death getting a sprained ankle.

However that wasn't the Griffins' last brush with Death as he's turned up numerous times over the years,

DID YOU KNOW?

DEATH DOESN'T HANDLE THE DEMISE OF CANINES, AS THERE'S A SPECIAL DOGGY GRIM REAPER TO DEAL WITH THAT.

most notably in 'Wasted Lives', where we discover being the Grim Reaper isn't the life of sex, drugs and rock 'n' roll you might expect. He's actually rather shy, unable to talk to women (which isn't necessarily a bad thing, as it turns out the woman

he fancies is so tedious that Death decides to kill her), and he still lives with his mother, who smothers him.

He's pretty self-conscious, partly because as a teenager he had a habit of killing any girl he was with (not that he let that stop him losing his virginity), and that being a rotting skeleton in a robe means he's completely minus an ass.

Actually he's a little obsessed with asses and carries a picture of Edward James Olmos's butt around with him! That may be part of his confused sexuality, as he's admitted he lost his gag reflex doing films he's not proud of.

He doesn't exactly have the greatest personality either, being rather sarcastic, blunt and rude.

Death does have his uses though, such as showing Peter his life without Lois and trying to make him appreciate her. When Peter travels to the past and screws up the present, he allows the fat man to repeatedly travel back to 1984 in order to put things right.

In the latest season he also shows Peter his life without alcohol, which perhaps surprisingly isn't that much better!

Just don't touch him though, or you'll end up dead as well!

DEATH'S MOTHER:
DEATH, PUT ON YOUR JACKET OR YOU'LL GET FROSTBITE!

DEATH: **I DON'T HAVE SKIN!**

DEATH'S MOTHER:
THAT'S 'CAUSE YOU DIDN'T EAT YOUR BEANS!

From: Death Lives

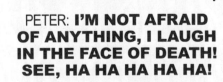

PETER: **I'M NOT AFRAID OF ANYTHING, I LAUGH IN THE FACE OF DEATH! SEE, HA HA HA HA HA!**

DEATH: **OH GREAT! THANKS A LOT! AS IF IT WASN'T ALREADY HARD ENOUGH TO FIT IN.**

From: Family Guy Viewer Mail #1

WHAT'S THE WORD?

THE BEST QUOTES OF LOIS GRIFFIN

"LOOK MEG – A: EAR SEX IS JUST UNNATURAL, AND B: HOW DO I SAY THIS, VAGINAL INTERCOURSE IS... IT'S JUST TOPS! IT'S THE BEE'S KNEES, MEG. OH, WHEN YOU RATTLE IT AROUND JUST RIGHT, OH MY GOD! I MEAN, YOU REMEMBER WHEN WE HAD THAT OLD CAR WITH THE BAD SHOCKS, AND I USED TO TAKE THE OLD DIRT ROAD ON PURPOSE!"

From: Prick Up Your Ears

MEG: MOM, IS SODOMY ILLEGAL IF YOU'RE JEWISH?

LOIS: I HOPE SO, MEG. I REALLY DO.

From: Family Goy

"STEWIE, IF YOU CAN HEAR ME, HEAD FOR MEG'S BUTT!"

From: Petergeist

CHRIS: And here's the broken condom that led to my birth!

LOIS: And the resulting lawsuit bought us this house. You're our favourite mistake.

From: Emission Impossible

LOIS: PETER, I CARE AS MUCH ABOUT THE SIZE OF YOUR PENIS AS YOU CARE ABOUT THE SIZE OF MY BREASTS.

PETER: OH, MY GOD!

From: And The Weiner Is...

"Chris, you can't join the Army! Besides, the Army's weak. Now the Marines, those are the men you wanna f**k"

From: Saving Private Brian

"OH, CHRIS, MY BABY! I'M TELLING YOU, PETER, I NEVER SHOULD HAVE LET HIM OUT OF MY STOMACH!."

From: Jungle Love

BRIAN: I can't believe you're serving a three year sentence, it seems so harsh.

LOIS: Well, the only upside is that it's given me time to think about why I ended up in here. I guess I was stealing because I was so sick of the same old routine. I felt like I had a void in my life, like there was a secret hole in me...

QUAGMIRE: Oh God!

LOIS: ...and I was trying to fill that hole with all kinds of expensive objects, and things...

QUAGMIRE: Oh god!

LOIS: ...and I felt wonderful with all those things filling that hole.

QUAGMIRE: Oh God!

LOIS: I did this to myself, so I'm just gonna have to lay back and let the penal system teach me a lesson.

QUAGMIRE: That one is also sexual.

From: Breaking Out Is Hard To Do

(ABOUT PETER) THIS IS A MAN WHO THINKS THE PLURAL OF GOOSE IS SHEEP.

From: Running Mates

LOIS: Peter, my God, you look terrible. What happened?

PETER: I was raped.

LOIS: What?

PETER: Dr. Hartman violated me. He took my innocence.

LOIS: W-What?

[Peter whispers in her ear]

LOIS: Peter, that's a prostate exam. It's an important part of a physical for men your age.

PETER: You sound just like him!

LOIS: F**kin' idiot.

From: Stewie Love Lois

MEG: (On first seeing their new Southern US house) Eww, we're going to be living here?

LOIS: Now come on Meg, I bet if we fixed it up a little, it could be a piece of crap.

From: To Love And Die In Dixie

"Hey there, sweetie! I got a wax this morning and, let's just say, you're cleared for landing!"

From: Model Misbehavior

"I'm pretty sure our washing machine is pregnant. I don't even know how that's scientifically possible!"

From: German Guy

"Kids, we just have to learn to accept this. Like one of those stories on Dateline where a family member suffers a horrible accident and becomes a burden on everybody. Sure, they pretend to be happy, but they're dead inside, they're dead. And that'll be our lives."

From: Viewer Mail #1

THE ULTIMATE Family Guy quiz PART 2

1. What was the name of the Swansons's son, who was killed in Iraq?

2. How does Peter's toy factory boss, Mr. Weed, die?

3. After Mr. Weed dies, the toy factory closes. What faux-Medieval job does Peter briefly have immediately afterwards?

4. When Peter becomes a deep sea fisherman, what is the name of the legendary man-eating fish he's told to avoid?

5. What's the name of the Southern US town where the Griffins live while in the FBI witness protection programme, in the episode 'To Love and Die in Dixie'?

6. In the same episode, what type of animal is the local school's top student?

7. In 'Screwed The Pooch', what's the name of Carter Pewterschmidt's prized dog that Brian thinks he's gotten pregnant?

8. And what does the judge tell Brian he needs to do in order to have custody of his puppies?

9. What is the name of Peter's African-American slave great-great-great-great Grandfather?

10. In the episode where Peter finds out about his slave ancestor, what African name does the Griffin patriarch try to adopt?

11. In the episode 'Ready, Willing And Disabled', which 'Golden Girls' star plays Peter in the fictitious TV movie, 'Rolling Courage: The Joe Swanson Story'?

12. What does Stewie want for Christmas from Santa in 'A Very Special Family Guy Freakin' Christmas'?

Here's the second part of the greatest test of Family Guy knowledge ever conceived. Make sure your brain is revved up to answer questions on everything from Peter's toy factory boss, to the reason why Stewie once ran away to Europe.

13. In the same episode, what is it that sends Lois over the edge and on a rampage through town, having got fed up with her family's lazy attitude to Christmas preparations?

14. What is the name of the elderly shut-in Brian falls in love with after hearing her sing Habanera from the opera Carmen, in the episode 'Brian Wallows and Peter's Swallows'?

15. And why does Brian meet the old lady in the first place?

16. What's the name of the family of nudists the Griffins occasionally bump into?

17. In 'From Method To Madness', what is the name of the girl Stewie briefly has a stage act with (and returns in a later episode to become his fake wife)?

18. The actress Jennifer Love Hewitt is revealed to be the niece of which recurring characters in the episode 'Stuck Together, Torn Apart'?

19. In 'Wasted Talent' what instrument does Lois discover Peter can play, but only when he's drunk?

20. In 'Road To Europe', which fictional BBC children's TV show does Stewie run away from home to try and be part of?

21. What's the name of the band KISS's five-date New England tour in the episode 'Road To Europe'?

22. In the same episode, what sort of animal do Stewie and Brian nearly have to cut open and sleep inside of, when they get lost in the desert?

23. In the 'No Bones About It' segment of the episode 'Family Guy Viewer Mail #1', what are three wishes Peter asks the Genie for?

24. In the 'Supergriffins' segment of the same episode, what is Meg's superhero power?

25. Why does Peter want Chris to become Jewish in 'When You Wish Upon a Weinstein'?

TURN TO PAGE 140 FOR THE ANSWERS

SEASON 3 & 4

HIGHTLIGHTS

 PTV

Despite being desperate to watch the Emmys, Peter is made to go and watch Meg's play at school.

This means he misses "a moment in television history," when a 'trouser malfunction' causes David Hyde Pierce's testicles to be exposed. The FCC (Federal Communications Commission) decides they must respond to this by censoring all television and removing anything even vaguely suggestive from the air.

Peter responds by setting up his own channel – PTV – dedicated to everything that's a little bit rude, such as The Peter Griffin Side Boob Hour. The FCC shuts down PTV, declaring it illegal. Federal agents then decide they must censor real life, with agents using air horns beeping out foul language, and stopping anyone from having sex. It's up to the Griffins to stop the fellas at the freakin' FCC!

TOP MOMENT: QUAGMIRE FAINTING AFTER HEARING PETER SCREAM: "I LIKE EATING RED CARPET!"

TOP QUOTE: "HOW 'BOUT THAT SIDE BOOB? HUH? THAT TURN YOU ON? WELL, IT SHOULDN'T, BECAUSE THAT'S MY SIDE BOOB. GOOD NIGHT, EVERYBODY." PETER

 **The Thin White Line**

After getting stuck in an emotional rut, Brian stumbles into a job as a drug-sniffing dog for the local police department.

Initially successful, being around all that cocaine begins to take its toll and Brian becomes a drug-fiend, treats his family like crap and dates a crack whore. The Griffins intervene and Brian agrees to go to rehab.

It turns out that rehab is too nice and Peter is so impressed that he decides to stay and take a vacation, pretending he's an addict too. Peter's obnoxious behaviour ends up with Brian being sucked into his antics, resulting in them both getting kicked out.

TOP MOMENT: WHILE HE'S A POLICE DOG, BRIAN INSISTS A CLASS FULL OF KIDS HAS SOMETHING TO DO WITH DRUGS, WHICH THE REST OF THE FORCE THINKS IS RIDICULOUS, UNTIL THEY'RE REVEALED TO BE COLOMBIAN MIDGETS!

TOP QUOTE: "OH, SPLENDID, FIDO MCCOKE-FIEND IS HOME." STEWIE

Emission Impossible

After witnessing the birth of Lois's sister's baby, Peter and Lois decide they want to try for another child.

Meg and Chris appear okay with this but Stewie is less than impressed. The maniacal infant vows to do whatever he can to prevent his parents conceiving. He uses a shrinking ray he's invented to make him and his spaceship-like vessel small enough to go inside Peter's body, in an attempt to destroy all his father's sperm.

While most of the sperm are easy fodder for Stewie's death rays, there's one that's more than a worthy adversary – Bertram – who's just as evil as Stewie. The two fight before Stewie comes to realise that Bertram could be a great ally if he were ever to be born. He decides conception must happen.

TOP MOMENT: IN ORDER TO PREVENT HIS PARENTS CONCEIVING, STEWIE BUILDS A ROBOT OF HIS FATHER. THE MECHANICAL MAN INSULTS LOIS AND THEN FALLS OUT OF THE WINDOW.

TOP QUOTE: "IT'S A BEAUTIFUL BABY GIRL... BUT THIS GIRL HAS A PENIS. OH WELL, WE'LL SOON SORT THAT OUT." PETER

PETARDED

After winning at Trivial Pursuit – even though he was answering question from the Pre-School Edition, whilst everyone else was doing the normal version – Peter becomes convinced he's a genius.

Brian challenges him to apply for an award given only to people with massive intellects. When the results come back, it turns out Peter is technically mentally retarded.

While this initially causes him distress, Peter soon realises that if people think you're retarded, you can get away with all sorts of things, such as peeping at women in the ladies room.

His antics result in Lois being hospitalised after Peter accidentally pours boiling fat over her. Child Protective Services then takes the kids away, as they feel Peter is mentally unfit to look after them. Can he get them back?

TOP MOMENT: PETER BEING ANNOYED AT HAVING TO WEAR WATER-WINGS IN ORDER TO EAT SOUP, BEFORE ALMOST DROWNING IN THE BOWL

TOP QUOTE: "ATTENTION ALL RESTAURANT CUSTOMERS. TESTICLES. THAT IS ALL." PETER

Peter Griffin: Husband, Father... Brother?

After Chris starts talking 'street' (which Peter initially think is Chris speaking in tongues, so he tries to exorcise him), Cleveland suggest Peter teach his son about his heritage, so he feels less inclined to adopt other cultures.

Peter researches his family tree, where he discovers his great-great-great-great-grandfather, Nate Griffin, was black. After trying to come to terms with his new identity and what it means to have suddenly become a black man, things get even more awkward when it's discovered that Lois's family, the Pewterschmidts, once owned Nate.

Peter demands reparations from his father-in-law, but after squandering the money rather than sharing it with the black community, he finds himself ostracised by everyone.

TOP MOMENT: THE SUBPLOT, WHICH INVOLVES STEWIE BELIEVING CHEERLEADERS HAVE MIND CONTROL ABILITIES BECAUSE OF THE WAY THEY WHIP AUDIENCES INTO A FRENZY.

TOP QUOTE: "HEAVENS, IT APPEARS MY WEE-WEE HAS BEEN STRICKEN WITH RIGOR MORTIS." STEWIE

WHAT'S THE WORD?

THE BEST QUOTES OF MEG GRIFFIN

MEG: I wanted to thank you for being so great to me, so I baked you a pie.

BRIAN: Oh wow. Hey that looks delicious. Mmm, oh, this is good. What's in there?

MEG: Well, there's some apples and some cinnamon... and my hair.

BRIAN: What?

MEG: My hair's in the pie Brian. And now, it's inside of you. Part of me is inside of you, Brian. Do you feel me, Brian? Do feel me inside of you?

From: Barely Legal

LOIS: I'M GONNA BECOME A MODEL.

PETER: HEY, THAT'S FANTASTIC, LOIS. AND I'LL PLEASURE MYSELF TO YOUR PHOTOS.

CHRIS: ME TOO.

MEG: ME TOO.

PETER: OH, GOD, MEG, THAT'S SICK. THAT'S YOUR MOTHER!

MEG: I'M JUST TRYING TO FIT IN.

PETER: GET OUT. GET OUT OF THIS HOUSE.

From: Model Misbehavior

CHRIS: My dad's smarter than your dad.

MEG: We have the same dad, idiot!

CHRIS: Yeah, but mine's smarter!

From: Petarded

MEG: Mom, Dad, am I ugly?

LOIS: Oh, of course not, sweetie.

PETER: Yeah, where'd you get a stupid idea like that?

MEG: Craig Hoffman.

PETER: Craig Hoffman said that? Well, he's a sharp kid. You may be ugly.

MEG: So is, uh, is this like the part where you guys have your way with me?

ROBBER 1: What?

MEG: You know, where I'm like helpless, and you guys take turns... you know?

ROBBER 1: Oh, no! Oh, God! Oh, no, no no no!

ROBBER 2: [from another room] What'd she say?

ROBBER 1: She asked if we were gonna have our way with her.

ROBBER 2: Ewww!

MEG: No, seriously, I won't scream or anything.

ROBBER 1: No! No, I, I, no, no sale!

MEG: C'mon! I'm pretty!

From: Untitled Family Guy History

LOIS: OH LOOK, MEG, IT'S YOUR LITTLE BABY BOOTIES, OH AND YOUR LITTLE BRONZED HAT... AND YOUR TAIL.

MEG: MY WHAT?!

LOIS: NOTHING.

From: Fore, Father

"You can't sell me you fat son of a bitch!"

From: 8 Simple Rules for Buying My Teenage Daughter

FAMILY GUY IS JUSTLY FAMED FOR ITS MUSICAL NUMBERS, SOMETIMES CREATING NEW VERSIONS OF OLD SONGS AND OTHER TIMES COMING UP WITH INCREDIBLE, ALL-NEW ORIGINAL TUNES. IF YOU'VE EVER WANTED TO SING-ALONG WITH SOME OF THESE GREAT SONGS, HERE'S YOUR CHANCE, AS WE'VE GOT THE LYRICS FOR THE BEST OF FAMILY GUY'S MUSICAL NUMBERS. SO WARM UP YOUR VOCALS CHORDS AND GET READY TO SING!

SING-ALONG-A Family Guy

ALL I WANT FOR CHRISTMAS

CHRISTMAS GETS ITS OWN 'ROAD TO...' EPISODE IN SEASON 9 OF FAMILY GUY, WITH BRIAN AND STEWIE OFF TO SEE SANTA, BUT BEFORE THAT THE RESIDENTS OF SPOONER STREET WANT TO TELL US THEIR HOLLY JOLLY HOPES FOR THE FESTIVE SEASON.

PETER: Jessica Biel and Megan Fox Wearin' nothin' but their socks, is all I really want for Christmas this year.

BRIAN: Well, that's just not practical.

LOIS: Spending a week in Mexico with some black guys and some blow,is all I really want for Christmas this year.

PETER: Aw, that sounds terrific. How about you, kids?

CHRIS: I would like a pair of skates, Then I'd go out skating, But I really don't know how to skate. Ha-ha!

MEG: I want a Lexus all in pink, And a dad who doesn't drink.

PETER: Oh, and that reminds me, twelve kegs of beer.

THE GRIFFINS: All these happy wishes, And lots of Christmas cheer, Is all I really want this year.

BRIAN: Santa's got his work cut out.

PETER: Oh, we ain't even gotten started yet.

LOIS: I wanna tour the Spanish coast.

PETER: Lunch with Michael Landon's ghost.

PETER AND LOIS: Is all I really want for Christmas this year.

LOIS: Wait, what?

PETER: Forget it. Keep goin'.

CHRIS: Jennifer Garner in my bed.

MEG: Softer voices in my head.

CHRIS AND MEG: Is all I really want for Christmas this year.

STEWIE: Yellow cake uranium. Never mind the reason. Also Chutes and Ladders and a ball.

BRIAN: Doesn't this seem like too much stuff?

PETER: Poo on you! It's not enough!

STEWIE: Buddy boy, I got your Christmas right here. [grabs his crotch]

THE GRIFFINS: All these happy wishes, And lots of Christmas cheer, Is all I really want this year.

BRIAN: I'm just saying it seems a bit excessive.

LOIS: Oh, get off your soapbox, Brian, it's Christmas.

PETER: And Christmas is about gettin'. Everyone in town knows that.

QUAGMIRE: Japanese girls with no restraint, just to choke me till I faint Is all I really want for Christmas this year. Ooh, giggity!

BONNIE: Platinum-plated silverware.

JOE: Just one day when kids don't stare.

BONNIE AND JOE: Is all I really want for Christmas this year.

MORT: If you put a Christmas tree In the public airport, I will go to court and sue your ass! Happy holiday!

MAYOR WEST: Wouldn't I love a Tinkertoy?

HERBERT: And a little drummer boy. He can either tap his drum or my rear.

MAYOR WEST, HERBERT AND MORT: All these happy wishes And lots of Christmas cheer Is all I really want this year.

TOM TUCKER: I want a golden moustache comb.

ANGELA: And some spermicidal foam.

TOM TUCKER AND ANGELA: That's all I really want for Christmas this year.

CARTER: I want a brand new pitching wedge.

CONSUELA: I would like more Lemon Pledge.

CARTER AND CONSUELA: That's all I really want for Christmas this year.

BRUCE: I just want a wedding ring From someone named Jeffrey.

JILLIAN: I just want some coloured Easter eggs.

CARL: I want a Blu-Ray of The Wiz.

BELLGARDE: We don't know what Christmas is.

TOMAK: We have something else called Gishgemfloofneer!

EVERYONE: All these happy wishes, And lots of Christmas cheer, Is all I really want this year.

WE'RE OFF ON THE ROAD TO RHODE ISLAND

From: Road To Rhode Island

A PARODY OF THE NUMBERS FROM THE CLASSIC 'ROAD TO...' MOVIES, STEWIE AND BRIAN DECIDE THEY NEED TO EXPRESS WHAT A GREAT TIME THEY'VE HAD CROSSING THE COUNTRY TOGETHER.

BOTH: We're off on the road to Rhode Island. We're having the time of our lives.

STEWIE: Take it dog...

BRIAN: We're quite the pair of partners, Just like Thelma and Louise. 'Cept your not six feet tall.

STEWIE: Yes, and your breasts don't reach your knees.

BRIAN: Give it time.

BOTH: We're off on the road to Rhode Island. We're certainly going in style.

BRIAN: I'm with an intellectual, who craps inside his pants.

STEWIE: How dare you. At least I don't leave urine stains on all the household plants.

BRIAN: Oh, pee jokes.

BOTH: We've travelled a bit and we've found, Like a masochist in Newport We're Rhode Island bound.

BRIAN: Crazy travel conditions, huh?

STEWIE: First class or no class.

BRIAN: Careful with that joke, it's an antique.

BOTH: We're off on the road to Rhode Island. We're not going to stop 'til we're there.

BRIAN: Maybe for a beer. Whatever dangers we may face, We'll never fear or cry.

STEWIE: That's right. Until we're syndicated Fox will never let us die (Please!).

BOTH: We're off on the road to Rhode Island, The home of the old campus swing.

BRIAN: We may pick up some college girls, And picnic on the grass

STEWIE: We'd tell you more, but we would have the censors on our ass (Yikes!).

BOTH: We're off on the road to Rhode Island We certainly do get around.

Like a bunch of renegade pilgrims who are thrown out of Plymouth Colony...
We're Rhode Island Bound
Or like a group of College Freshmen who were rejected by Harvard and forced to go to Brown...
We're Rhode Island bound!

I NEED A JEW

From: When You Wish Upon A Weinstein

THIS SONG WAS SO CONTROVERSIAL THAT IT WAS PARTIALLY RESPONSIBLE FOR FOX INITIALLY DECIDING NOT TO AIR THE EPISODE IN THE US, DUE TO CONCERNS IT WOULD BE SEEN AS ANTI-SEMITIC (WHICH WAS SOMEWHAT IRONIC, AS THE PERSON WHO WROTE THE SONG IS JEWISH).

PETER:
Nothing else has worked so far,
So I'll wish upon a star,
Wondrous dancing speck of light,
I need a Jew.

Lois makes me take the rap,
Cause our checkbook looks like crap,
Since I can't give her a slap,
I need a Jew.

Where to find, a Baum
or Stien of Stein?
To teach me how to whine
and do my taxes.

Though by many they're abhorred,
Hebrew people I've adored,
Even though they killed my lord,
I need a Jew!

(A knock at the door)

MAX: (speaking)
Hi, my name's Max Weinstein. My car just broke down, may I use you phone?

PETER:
Now my troubles are all through, I have a Jew!

DID YOU KNOW?

In 'The Courtship of Stewie's Father', Herbert sings 'Somewhere That's Green', from the musical Little Shop Of Horrors. The scene is a shot-for-shot remake of that song from the 1986 film version of the musical, but with Herbert and Chris replacing Ellen Greene and Rick Moranis.

I'VE GOT A LITTLE LIST

From: Lois Kills Stewie

A PARODY OF A SONG FROM GILBERT & SULLIVAN'S THE MIKADO, I'VE GOT A LITTLE LIST ALLOWS STEWIE TO VENT HIS FRUSTRATION WITH THE WORLD, AND TELL US WHO HE THINKS WOULDN'T BE MISSED IF HE ELIMINATED THEM. THE SONG WAS CUT FOR TIME WHEN THE EPISODE WAS FIRST SHOWN ON AMERICAN TV BUT HAS BEEN INCLUDED ON THE DVD VERSION.

STEWIE: As someday it may happen that a victim must be found, I've got a little list, I've got a little list Of society offenders who might well be underground, And who never would be missed, who never would be missed.

There's the white kid with the baggy clothes who's talking like he's black, The girl you date who doesn't get the jokes in Caddyshack, The Asian guy who cuts in front of every single line, And Britney Spears for accidentally showing her vagine, And Bill O'Reilly's ineffective dermatologist. They'd none of them be missed, they'd none of them be missed.

SECRET SERVICE MEN: He's got them on the list, He's got them on the list, And they'd none of them be missed, They'd none of them be missed.

STEWIE: There's the guy behind the news reporter waving like a fool, And Senator Bill Frist, I've got him on the list. And the fat kid smiling warmly while he's peeing in the pool. He never would be missed, he never would be missed.

There's the foul-smelling boy who comes to school in camouflage, And every bleeding member of the cast of Entourage, And while we're on the subject, HBO deserves a whack For ending The Sopranos with a f****g cut to black! And guys who when you shake their hand just bump you with their fist. I don't think they'd be missed. I'm sure they'd not be missed.

SECRET SERVICE MEN: He's got them on the list, He's got them on the list, And they'd none of them be missed, They'd none of them be missed.

STEWIE: There's the guy who sits beside you and keeps farting on the plane And Shakira's lyricist. I've got him on the list. And the smarty on Thanksgiving who says, "It's the tryptophan!" He never would be missed, he never would be missed.

There's the blonde who tells you loudly with a voice just like a knife, "You know, someone should do a sitcom based around my life!" The guy who watched The Simpsons back in 1994 And won't admit the damn thing isn't funny anymore.

STEWIE AND SECRET SERVICE MEN: And anyone, and everyone... Who's ever Made me pissed!

SECRET SERVICE MEN: Made me pissed! Made me really, really pissed!

STEWIE: I've got them on the list. They'd none of them be missed.

SECRET SERVICE MEN: They'd be none, they'd be... They'd be none, they'd be none of them be missed. He's got them on the list, He's got them on the list, And they'd none of them be missed...

STEWIE: They'd none...

SECRET SERVICE MEN: None of them...

STEWIE & SECRET SERVICE MEN: Be Missed!

PROM NIGHT DUMPSTER BABY

From: Airport '07

LIKE I NEED A JEW, THIS WAS ONE OF THE MOST CONTROVERSIAL THINGS FAMILY GUY HAS EVER DONE, WITH A WHOLE SONG AND DANCE NUMBER POPULATED BY BABIES WHO'VE BEEN PLONKED IN A DUMPSTER SO THEIR MOTHERS CAN GO TO THE SCHOOL PROM. INSPIRED BY REAL CASES, IT SET A LOT OF REACTIONARY NERVES JANGLING, WHILE EVERYONE WITH A SENSE OF HUMOUR JUST THOUGHT IT WAS FUNNY.

BABY: I'm just a prom night dumpster baby,
I got no mom or dad. Prom night dumpster baby,
My story isn't long but boy it's awfully sad.

BACKUP BABIES: Ba-ba-ba-ba-ba-bum.

BABY: And though I came from a hole.

BACKUP BABIES: And though he came from a hole.

BABY: I'm singing right from the soul.

BACKUP BABIES: He's singing right from the soul.

BABY: My fanny needs a blanket,
And somebody to spank it.
I miss my Mom...

BACKUP BABIES: But she's at the prom.

ALL: So I'm a prom night dumpster baby.
Prom night dumpster baby.
Ba-ba-ba-ba-ba-ba-ba-bum.

BABY: And I'm takin' a stroll,

BACKUP BABIES: He's takin' a stroll,

BABY: I'm takin' a stroll,

BACKUP BABIES: He's takin' a stroll,

BABY: I'm takin' a stroll,

BACKUP BABIES: He's takin' a stroll.

BABY: Uh huh-huh-huh-huh. I'm takin' a stroll.

BACKUP BABIES: He's takin' a stroll.

BABY: I'm takin' a stroll.

YOU HAVE AIDS!

From: The Cleveland–Loretta Quagmire

NOT ONE TO SHY AWAY FROM CONTROVERSY IN MUSIC, FAMILY GUY SLIGHTLY GOT IT IN THE ARM FOR THE MUSICAL NUMBER YOU HAVE AIDS. PART OF A DELIBERATELY TASTELESS CUTAWAY GAG, IT FEATURES PETER AS PART OF A BARBERSHOP QUARTET WHO JUMP IN TO TELL AN UNSUSPECTING PATIENT ABOUT HIS RATHER UNFORTUNATE MEDICAL STATUS.

DR. HARTMAN: I don't know how to tell you this, Mr. Devanney, so I'll let these guys do it...

PETER: You have AIDS.

GROUP: Yes, you have AIDS.

PETER: I hate to tell you boy, that you have AIDS.

GROUP: You got the AIDS.

PETER: You may have caught it when you stuck that filthy needle in here (points to arm).

GROUP: Or maybe all that unprotected sex put you here.

PETER: It isn't clear.

ALL: But what we're certain of is...

PETER: You have AIDS.

GROUP: Yes, you have AIDS.

PETER: Not HIV...

ALL: but full-blown AIDS.

GROUP: Be sure that you see, that this is not HIV.

ALL: But full-blown AIDS.

BASS SOLO: I'm sorry, I wish it was something less serious.

ALL: But it's AIDS. You've got the AIDS.

DID YOU KNOW?

Many people were confused by a moment in the episode, 'It Takes a Village Idiot, and I Married One', where Happy Days actor Donny Most rises from the fog as ethereal voices sing his name. It's actually a reference to the musical Brigadoon, where a village comes into existence for just one day every hundred years.

THIS HOUSE IS FREAKIN' SWEET!

From: Peter, Peter, Caviar Eater

NOMINATED FOR AN EMMY, THIS WONDERFUL SONG, WHICH REFERENCES 'I THINK I'M GOING TO LIKE IT HERE' FROM ANNIE, IS ONE OF THE BIGGEST MUSICAL NUMBERS FAMILY GUY HAS EVER ATTEMPTED. IT APPEARS JUST AFTER THE GRIFFINS INHERIT A PALATIAL MANSION FROM LOIS'S FILTHY RICH AUNT, AND THE STAFF TURN OUT TO WELCOME PETER AND HIS FAMILY IN FINE MUSICAL STYLE.

SERVANTS: We only live to kiss your ass.

SEBASTIAN: Kiss it? Hell, we'll even wipe it for you!

SERVANTS: From here on in, it's Easy Street.

PETER: Any bars on that street?

SEBASTIAN: 24 happy hours a day.

PETER: Oh, boy!

SERVANTS: We'll stop Jehovah's at the gate.

GUARD: Can I see that pamphlet, sir? (Whacks Jehovah's Witness with the pamphlet).

PETER: My God, this house is freakin' sweet.

CHEF: I make brunch, Clive cooks lunch, each and every day.

BLAKE: Chocolate cake, a la Blake!

PETER: Hundred bucks, Blake is gay.

SERVANTS: We'll do the best we can with Meg.

MEG: Are you sayin' I'm ugly?

SERVANT: It doesn't matter, dear. You're rich now!

SERVANTS: We'll do your nails and rub your feet.

LOIS: Oh that's not necess-oh my.

SERVANTS: We'll do your homework every night.

CHRIS: It's really hard.

SEBASTIAN: That's why we got that Stephen Hawking guy.

PETER: My God, this house is freakin' sweet! Used to pass lots of gas; Lois ran away. Now we've got 30 rooms! Hello, beans. Goodbye, spray!

SERVANTS: We'd take a bullet just for you.

STEWIE: Oh, what a coincidence, I've got one.

LOIS: Stewie!

SERVANTS: Prepare to suck that golden teat. Now that you're stinking rich, we'll gladly be your bitch.

PETER: My god, this house is....

ALL: freakin' sweet! Welcome!

SERVANT: (talking) That's a wrap, people. Now let's get the hell out of here.

PETER: Wait a second, where you going?

SERVANT: The old bag only paid us up through the song.

LOIS: Well, we can just pick up after ourselves. After all, we'll only be here on weekends.

PETER: No no, Lois. It's time you started living like the piece of Schmidt you are.

LOIS: That's 'Pewterschmidt'.

PETER: Wait, you guys! You guys, you're all hired to be full time Griffin servants.

LOIS: Peter, where are we going to get the money to pay all these people?

PETER: Simple. I, eh, sold our house in Quahog.

LOIS: You sold our home?!

PETER: Surprise!

LOIS: Peter, how could you?

PETER: (Singing) I recognise that tone. Tonight I sleep alone.

ALL: But still this house is freakin' sweet!

DOWN SYNDROME GIRL

From: Extra Large Medium

THIS CONTROVERSIAL BUT EMMY-NOMINATED NUMBER COMES WHEN STEWIE IS HELPING CHRIS PREPARE FOR A DATE WITH ELLEN, WHO HAS DOWN SYNDROME. IT PARTLY SATIRISES MANY PEOPLE'S RATHER SIMPLISTIC IDEAS ABOUT PEOPLE WHO ARE DIFFERENT, SOMETHING WHICH CHRIS REALISES WHEN HE ACTUALLY GOES ON THE DATE!

STEWIE: You've got to
look your best tonight,
You tubby little parasite,
'Cause there's a lovely lady
and she's waiting for you.
And though her pretty face may seem
a special person's wettest dream,
Before you get to see it there
are things you must do.

We'll try a tie and boutonniere of yellow,
Or a rose that shows that
you're a classy fellow,
With the posh panache of
Jefferson at Monticello,
Busting out a mile with style.

I know you just can't wait to stare
at all that luscious orange hair,
But, boy, before you
touch a single curl,
You must impress
that ultra bloomin',
All-consumin',
poorly groomin'
Down Syndrome girl.

On any normal day
you reek as if you're
on a farting streak.
Your finger's up your
nose and you are
dripping with drool,
But if you want
a lady's love,
you're better off
by smelling of
a gentleman's cologne
instead of sneakers
and stool.

A squirt, a spurt of
something just for
Ellen, and you'll
see, that she
will find you so
compellin'.
And she does,
because the only

smell that she'll be smellin'
won't be coming from your bum.
You wanna take that little whore
and spin her on the dancing floor,
But boy, before you do a single twirl,
you must impress that effervescing,
self-possessing, no BS-ing
Down Syndrome girl.

Her eyes are emerald portals
to a secret land of love,
And her smile is like the
sweetest summer flower.
Her kiss is so inviting and her
hugs are so delighting,
And what makes them really nice
is that they've got a little spice,
Because they're tighter than a vice
and they go on for an hour.

My boy, between the two of us,
we'll get you on that shorty bus
and then you're gonna
take it for a whirl.

Now go impress that super-thrilling.
wish-fulfilling, Yoo-Hoo spilling,
ultra-swinging, boner-bringing,
gaily singing, dingalinging,
stupefying, fortifying, as of Monday,
shoelace tying, stimulating,
titillating, kitty-cat impersonating,
mega-rocking, pillow-talking,
just a little crooked walking,
coyly pouting, booby-sprouting,
for some reason always shouting,
fascinating, captivating, happiness
and joy creating...
Down Syndrome Girl!

YOU'VE GOT A LOT TO SEE!

From: Brian Wallows And Peter's Swallows

WHILE SEVERAL FAMILY GUY MUSICAL NUMBERS HAVE BEEN NOMINATED FOR EMMYS IN THE 'OUTSTANDING MUSIC AND LYRICS' CATEGORY, 'YOU'VE GOT A LOT TO SEE!' IS THE ONLY ONE TO HAVE WON. AFTER FALLING FOR THE ELDERLY PEARL BURTON – WHO HASN'T BEEN OUT OF HER HOUSE FOR DECADES – BRIAN EMBARKS ON AN ELABORATE MUSICAL NUMBER TO CONVINCE PEARL THE OUTSIDE WORLD IS WORTH SEEING.

BRIAN: The 60s brought the hippie breed, And decades later things have changed indeed. We lost the values but we kept the weed. You've got a lot to see.

The Reagan years, have laid the frame for movies stars to play the White House game. We're not too far from voting Feldman/Haim. You've got a lot to see.

The town of Vegas has got a different face, 'cause it's a family place with lots to do. Where in the 50s a man could mingle with scores of all the seediest whores, well now his children can too.

You've heard it from the canine's mouth, the country's changed, that is except the South, and you'll agree no one really knows, my dear lady friend just quite how it all will end. So hurry, 'cause you've got a lot to see.

The baldness gene was cause for dread, but that's a fear that you can put to bed. They'll shave your ass and glue it on your head. You've got a lot to see.

The PC-age has moved the bar, a word like "redneck" is a step too far. The proper term is "country music star". You've got a lot to see.

Our flashy cell phones make people mumble, "Gee whiz... look how important he is, his life must rule!" You'll get a tumour, but on your surgery day, the doc will see it and say, "Wow, you must really be cool!"

TOM TUCKER: There's lots of things you may have missed.

MAYOR WEST: Like Pee Wee and his famous wrist.

CLEVELAND: Or Sandy Duncan's creepy phony eye.

NEIL GOLDMAN: That awesome Thundercats cartoon.

DIANE SIMMONS: Neil Armstrong landing on the moon.

MEG GRIFFIN: Neil Armstrong? Wait, was he the trumpet guy?

BRIAN: So let's go see the USA, they'll treat you right unless you're black or gay or Cherokee. But you can forgive the world and its flaws, and follow me there because you've still got a hell of a lot to see. You've got a lot to see!

THE ULTIMATE Family guy quiz

PART 3

1. What fictional Mel Gibson-directed sequel does Peter try to prevent from ever being released, in the episode 'North By North Quahog'?

2. In 'Fast Times at Buddy Cianci Jr. High', Lois believes Chris has murdered the husband of his seductive teacher, Mrs. Lockhart. Who actually did the killing?

3. What world record does Peter try to break in 'Blind Ambition', which causes him to lose his sight?

4. On which live television show does Meg lose her virginity in 'Don't Make Me Over'?

5. Who does Loretta Brown sleep with, which causes her and Cleveland Brown to split up and get divorced?

6. In 'Petarded', who takes custody of the Griffin kids, after they're taken away from Peter?

7. What's the name of Chris' talking pimple in the episode 'Brian The Bachelor'?

8. What superhero character does Lois dress up as, in order to try and seduce Neil Goldman in '8 Simple Rules For Dating My Teenage Daughter'?

9. What part of Quahog do the Griffins hide out in after breaking Lois from jail in 'Breaking Out Is Hard To Do'?

10. After whom does Peter want to rename James Woods Regional High School in 'Peter's Got Woods'?

11. What university did Brian drop out of, shortly before graduating?

12. What's the name of Lois's newly found but homicidal brother in 'Fat Guy Strangler'?

13. And which famous actor provided his voice?

14. Which singer do Brian and Stewie start crooning with in 'Brian Sings and Swings'?

15. In 'Patriot Games', what is the name of the terrible London-based American Football team Peter gets sold to?

16. What's the name of the woman Quagmire marries (who was initially a maid Peter won on a quiz show), in the episode 'I Take Thee, Quagmire'?

17. What was Lois and Peter's pot-fuelled band called, which they started in the 1970s and resurrected in the episode 'Deep Throats'?

18. Brian's gay cousin is called what?

19. In 'Stewie Loves Lois', what legitimate medical procedure does Peter undergo, which he interprets as Dr. Hartman raping him?

20. What was 'Dingo and the Baby', in the episode 'Mother Tucker'?

21. Which recurring gag first makes an appearance in the fifth season episode, 'Hell Comes To Quahog'?

22. In 'Saving Private Brian', what's the name of the goth band Chris sings with?

23. After the Opal Ring Crusade makes them promise to abstain, what substitute sexual activity do the kids of Quahog come up with, in the episode 'Prick Up Your Ears'?

24. What is the title of the terrible 'chick flick' Peter directs in 'Chick Cancer'?

25. In 'Barely Legal', why does Joe say he can't go to South America with the rest of the police force to search for a character from the film Romancing The Stone?

TURN TO PAGE 140 FOR THE ANSWERS

TOP 5 EPISODES

SEASON 5 & 6

HIGHTLIGHTS

 5 **Stewie Loves Lois**

After Lois fixes his teddy Rupert, Stewie is so overwhelmed with gratitude that he completely changes his mind about his mother and decides he loves her dearly.

Stewie's change in attitude becomes incredibly demanding. Lois is so worn down by his neediness that she dreams of killing him. Brian convinces Lois she needs to break Stewie's over-dependence, but the infant is not one to be ignored.

Peter is horrified after getting a prostate test result and is convinced the doctor has raped him. He takes Dr. Hartman to court to get his licensed revoked. When Peter discovers he has a problem up his bum, he can't find a doctor who will touch him due to his lawsuit.

TOP MOMENT: PETER TRYING TO FORCE DR. HARTMAN TO GIVE HIM AN EXAM, BY DRESSING AS A DELIVERY MAN WITH A BOX TIED TO HIS ASS.

TOP QUOTE: "IF IT'S GALE-FORCE PEEING YE BE DOIN' IT COULD MEAN YOU'VE GOT BARNACLES ON YOUR PROSTATE. BEST HAVE SICK BAY CHECK BELOW YOUR DECKS." SEAMUS

 4 **Chick Cancer**

After getting introduced to chick flicks, Peter decides to make his own, called Steel Vaginas.

Peter is not the most competent of directors and doesn't even realise that if Joe is in a wheelchair in real life, he won't be able to walk just because it says he does in a script. The resulting film isn't well received...

Stewie bumps into old flame Olivia and they start to date. After a mock wedding, their relationship soon begins to disintegrate into a bad marriage, filled with resentment, bickering and recriminations. Things come to a head when Olivia begins to see someone else behind Stewie's back.

TOP MOMENT: PETER SAYING HE WAS THE ORIGINAL PRETTY WOMAN, BEFORE WE SEE HIM IN THE JULIA ROBERTS ROLE.

TOP QUOTE: "LOIS, BEFORE I FOUND THESE MOVIES WOMEN ONLY MADE ME CRY THROUGH MY PENIS, NOW THEY MAKE ME CRY THROUGH MY EYES." PETER

3 Boys Do Cry

When Lois becomes the new church organist, she decides the whole family must go to church more regularly.

But when Stewie drinks too much Communion wine, he throws it up, convincing the people of Quahog he's possessed by the devil. With the priest wanting to exorcise him, the Griffins decide to go on the run and end up in Texas.

Stewie, disguised as a girl, is entered in the 'Little Miss Texas' pageant, Meg and Chris find new friends, and Peter becomes a cowboy. Even though Lois realises Quahog is no longer after them, she stays silent as she thinks Texas life is so wholesome – until the Texans discover Peter is retarded and decide to execute him.

TOP MOMENT: THE DISCOVERY OF THE SUPER-DEVIL, WHO'S WAY WORSE THAN THE NORMAL DEVIL AND HAS A MOTORBIKE!

TOP QUOTE: "IT'S ONE OF THEM QUEER-O-SEXUALS!" TEXAN MAN

2 McStroke

Peter grows a moustache and becomes obsessed with it. He's mistaken for a firefighter and ends up saving the owner of a burger restaurant from a blaze.

The man is so grateful he offers Peter free burgers for life. Peter eats so many that he has a stroke, leaving his left side entirely numb.

After recovering (thanks to stem cells), Peter decides to expose the meat industry, infiltrating the McBurgertown headquarters and slaughterhouse, and becoming friends with a genetically engineered cow who blows the whistle on the company's dodgy practices.

Stewie goes undercover as the cool new kid at Meg and Chris's high school, but gets more than he bargained for when the bitchy Connie DiMico sees the size of his penis.

TOP MOMENT: STEWIE GETS EVERYONE TO THINK CONNIE DIMICO IS A PAEDOPHILE, BY KISSING HER AND THEN STRIPPING AND CLAIMING THAT SHE'S SNOGGING A NUDE BABY.

TOP QUOTE: "OKAY, IF I WIN, AND YOU CAN'T DO IT, YOU HAVE TO PUT YOUR NOSE IN MEG'S HAT AND TAKE AN EIGHT-SECOND INHALE." BRIAN

1 PRICK UP YOUR EARS

After Lois catches Chris watching porn she discovers his school has no sex-education teacher and volunteers for the job.

She gets fired after parents are horrified that she's giving out factual information, instead of insisting on abstinence. The school responds by bringing in the 'Opal Ring Crusade', who convince the kids to be abstinent.

The youngsters find a novel way around this – ear sex – so they can still have sexual contact but in a way they don't think will anger God. Peter also gets caught up in the crusade and becomes abstinent.

Lois battles against this, although getting teens to give up abstinence turns out not to be great for Meg, as her boyfriend dumps her the moment he sees her naked.

TOP MOMENT: LOIS TRYING TO TURN-ON AN ABSTINENT PETER BY DRESSING UP AS RONALD MCDONALD'S FRIEND, THE PURPLE BLOB GRIMACE.

TOP QUOTE: "THAT'S CRAZY. YOU CAN'T GIVE UP SEX, YOU'VE GOT A RESPONSIBILITY. YOU SEE MEG, YOU'RE WHAT THEY CALL A 'PRACTICE GIRL'." PETER

WHAT'S THE WORD?

THE BEST QUOTES OF CHRIS GRIFFIN

MEG: CHRIS, GET OUT OF HERE! YOU'RE NOT ALLOWED IN MY ROOM!

CHRIS: I THOUGHT THAT WAS JUST WHEN YOU WERE ASLEEP.

From: The Son Also Draws

CHRIS: Meg won't stop pushing me!

MEG: Like I could, fat ass!

CHRIS: I'm not fat, I'm Rubenesque!

From: Emission Impossible

CHRIS: YOU'RE A DOG! YOU DON'T HAVE A SOUL!

BRIAN: OUCH.

From: North By North Quahog

MEG: I'm going to the mall later, maybe you can come and help me pick out some underwear.

BRIAN: Uhh, I don't think that's going to be a possibility, uhhh, I have plans, with Chris! Chris and I have plans this afternoon!

CHRIS: We do?

BRIAN: Yeah, yeah! We're doing that thing... we're doing that thing you usually do on a Thursday afternoon!

CHRIS: Masturbate?

BRIAN: That's it, that is what we're going to do together.

CHRIS: Well, maybe back to back, but I gotta tell you, I'm not 100% on this.

From: Barely Legal

CHRIS: I WAS GOING TO SCHOOL, AND THIS GUY WON'T LET ME.

PETER: OH YEAH? HIM AND WHAT ARMY?

CHRIS: THE US ARMY.

PETER: OH, THAT'S A GOOD ARMY.

From: E. Peterbus Unum

"WHAT GOOD IS MINING FOR NOSE GOLD IF YOU CAN'T SHARE IT WITH THE TOWNSPEOPLE?"

From: North by North Quahog

CHRIS: (ON THE PHONE) SO, UH, WHAT ARE YOU WEARING? WOW! I BET YOU COULD SEE RIGHT THROUGH THAT.

LOIS: CHRIS, WHO ARE YOU TALKING TO?

CHRIS: GRANDMA.

From: Brian In Love

"You know Anna, when I first saw you, I thought you were the most beautiful girl in the world. And now, all I wanna do is show you my innermost self, but I'm afraid you'll reject me because you won't like what you see. Or, that you'll see my scrotum and see that it has a seam on it and then you'll think I'm made up of two different guys that were sewn together, 'cause that's what I think happened."

From: Long John Peter

COP: (THINKING CHRIS IS SHOPLIFTING) ALL RIGHT SON, I'M GOING TO NEED THOSE TWO HAMS BACK.

CHRIS: HUH? I DON'T HAVE ANY HAMS!

COP: LIFT UP YOUR SHIRT, SON.

CHRIS: I NEED AN ADULT! I NEED AN ADULT!

COP: YOU'RE NOT A SHOPLIFTER, YOU'RE JUST A FAT KID! SORRY ABOUT THAT, FATTY FAT FATTY. HEY DOM HE'S JUST A FAT KID! AREN'T YOU, FATTY? YOU'RE JUST A BIG OL' FAT KID. HERE'S SOME CHOCOLATE, FATSO.

"OH NO! SOMEONE PEED IN MY PANTS!"

From: To Love And Die In Dixie

"MOM, I'M AFRAID IF I FALL ASLEEP, THE HURRICANE'S GONNA SNEAK UP ON ME AND GIVE ME A VASECTOMY."

From: One If By Clam, Two If By Sea

CHRIS ON WHAT HE WANTS FOR CHRISTMAS:

"I just want peace on Earth. That's better than being selfish like Meg, right? So I should get more than her."

From: A Very Special Family Guy Freakin' Christmas

LOIS: PETER, I NEED TO TALK TO YOU ABOUT YOUR SON.

PETER: WHICH ONE, THE FAT ONE OR THE FUNNY-LOOKING ONE?

CHRIS: (POINTING AT STEWIE) HA HA HA! DAD CALLED YOU FAT... WAIT.

From: The Courtship Of Stewie's Father

Behind The Scenes:

A BRIEF HISTORY OF

Family Guy

FAMILY GUY HAS BEEN ON OUR SCREENS FOR MORE THAN A DECADE AND THE GRIFFINS HAVE APPEARED IN MORE THAN 160 EPISODES OF ANIMATED MADNESS. BUT WHERE DID THE SHOW COME FROM? HOW HAS IT KEPT GOING? WHY WAS IT CANCELLED AND BROUGHT BACK TWICE?

The first episode of Family Guy aired in the US after Superbowl XXXIII on January 31, 1999. It attracted an audience of 22 million viewers, and more than a little controversy over its adult nature.

The history of Family Guy goes back a little before that, to a young Seth MacFarlane studying at the Rhode Island School of Design. Whilst there he created an animated short called 'The Life Of Larry' as his thesis film, based on a middle-aged man and his intellectual dog.

The follow-up, simply called 'Larry & Steve', caught the eye of the Fox Network in the States and they asked MacFarlane to develop an animated series based on the characters. The initial concept changed quite a lot and morphed into the entire Griffin family.

After their Superbowl debut, the first regular episode of the series aired on April 11, 1999. While at first it proved fairly popular, the number of viewers started to slide with many observers suggesting this was due to tough competition.

By the end of its second season, despite a very devoted core following, the series had dropped so far in the ratings that Fox wasn't certain whether they wanted to show Family Guy anymore and it was essentially cancelled. But the network then had a change of heart and decided to bring it back after a gap of nearly a year when a third season aired, starting in the summer of 2001.

Ratings didn't improve and by the end of that season Family Guy was rated 125 out of 158 shows on American network television, with only one of Fox's shows doing worse over the course of the season. Fox cancelled the show completely!

Then something rather unusual happened. After the rerun rights were sold to the Cartoon Network, the show started getting massive viewing figures on that channel, with ratings that were sometimes higher than when the show had first aired on normal TV, and nearly 300% higher than previously.

At the same time the Season 1 and 2 box set was released, selling nearly 400,000 copies within a month and more than 1.6 million copies in a year, to make it the biggest-selling TV box set ever.

After a second set of episodes on DVD sold another million copies, Fox took the almost unprecedented step of un-cancelling the series again. After a gap of more than three years, the first new episodes of the show aired on May 1, 2005. It was the first time ever that a cancelled series had been revived based on strong DVD sales and ratings for re-runs.

Since then the show has done better in the ratings and never been in danger of cancellation. With the show still selling massively on DVD, and its spin-off 'The Cleveland Show' now airing, Family Guy is one of the biggest TV shows around.

Family Guy - Too Hot For TV!

A few episodes of Family Guy have proven so controversial, that even after making them, the Fox network decided not to air them when it was initially planned.

When You Wish Upon A Weinstein

Plot: After screwing up the family finances, Peter decides he needs a Jew to help him cope better with money. One almost magically turns up, leading Peter to force him to help him out. The Griffin patriarch then decides Chris would get better grades in school if he were Jewish, and decides to convert his son, no matter what it takes.

Controversy: Fox decided not to show the episode as they were worried it was would be viewed as anti-Semitic. It was initially supposed to be shown in 2000, but didn't air in the US until 2003.

Partial Terms Of Endearment

Plot: Lois's old friend, Naomi, asks her to be a surrogate mother as she can't conceive naturally. Despite Peter's objections, Lois goes ahead with the fertilised egg implantation and is soon pregnant. Peter's still not keen and tries to get Lois to miscarry. However when Naomi and her husband die in a car crash, Lois is left with a decision as to whether to carry on the pregnancy, which becomes more difficult when Peter suddenly becomes stridently anti-abortion.

Controversy: While Fox allowed the Family Guy team to produce the episode, they felt the subject matter was too controversial, and so it didn't air in the US. The episode instead premiered in the UK in 2010.

Peterotica

Plot: After finding an erotic book disappointing, Peter starts writing his own naughty stories. When he gets money from his father-in-law, Carter, Peter starts publishing his tale. However a driver crashes while listening to some Peterotica on tape, and the resulting lawsuit leaves Carter destitute. Peter decides to teach his father-in-law how to be a regular guy.

Controversy: A brief gag in the episode featured American comedian Carol Burnett as her 'charlady' character, working as a janitor in an adult store. Burnett sued the show, saying the episode violated her publicity rights. A judge dismissed the case, saying parody was protected under US copyright law.

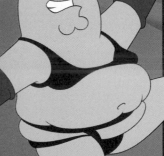

About The CAST

Seth MacFarlane

VOICES: Peter, Stewie, Brian

Raised in Kent, Connecticut, Seth MacFarlane studied animation at the Rhode Island School of Design. While there he created his thesis film 'The Adventures Of Larry'. The short impressed Hannah-Barbera, who encouraged him to move to LA and work for them. When Fox saw his follow-up to 'The Adventures Of Larry', called 'Larry & Steve', they asked him to develop it into a prospective series, which became Family Guy. When the show was picked up, MacFarlane was only 24, making him one of the youngest-ever executive producers in American TV.

As well as creating the series, MacFarlane voices Peter, Stewart, Brian, Quagmire, Seamus, Tom Tucker, Carter Pewterschmidt and others (he's also Stan Smith and Roger the alien in American Dad and Tim the Bear in The Cleveland Show).

He's won two Emmys for his work on Family Guy, one for 'Outstanding Voice-over Performance' for playing Stewie, and another for 'Outstanding Music And Lyrics' for the song 'You've Got A Lot To See' from the episode 'Brian Wallows and Peter's Swallows'.

SETH FACTS

* His sister is Rachael MacFarlane, who voices Hayley in American Dad.
* He was meant to be on one of the planes that crashed into the World Trade Center, but a mix up with timings meant he missed the flight.
* Plays the piano.
* He's a fan of Rex Harrison, and based Stewie's voice on the actor.

Alex Borstein

VOICES: Lois

Born and raised in the Chicago suburbs, Alex Borstein got into comedy whilst in college and in graduate school with ACME Comedy Theater. After some small TV roles, working in advertising and doing some TV writing, Borstein scored a role as one of the players of the late night sketch comedy show, MADtv.

It was while she was on that show that she was introduced to Seth MacFarlane, and recorded the voice for the pilot of Family Guy. When the show was picked up for air, she continued her role as the Griffin matriarch, and also voices the likes of Barbara Pewterschmidt and many of the other female characters.

Borstein has also done a lot of writing on the show, with Seth MacFarlane saying she helped expand the female characters, which the largely male writers had difficulty doing. She's also appeared in The Lizzie Maguire Movie, Catwoman, Bad Santa, Good Night And Good Luck, and Killers.

ALEX FACTS

* She was cast as Sookie St. James in Gilmore Girls, but couldn't take the part because of her MADtv contract. The role went to Melissa McCarthy.
* Her hubby, Jackson Douglas, is best known for playing Jackson Belleville on Gilmore Girls.
* She went with Halle Berry to pick up the her Worst Actress gong for Catwoman at the Razzies.

Seth Green

VOICES: Chris

When Family Guy started airing in 1999, Seth Green was probably the most famous of the voice artists, as he'd been playing Oz in Buffy The Vampire Slayer since 1997. Even by then he was a bit of a screen veteran, having scored his first TV role at the tender age of ten.

By the time he started working on Family Guy, he'd already appeared in My Stepmother Is An Alien, Pump Up The Volume, Can't Hardly Wait, and Austin Powers: International Man Of Mystery, as Dr. Evil's son, Scott, as well as numerous TV shows.

As well as Chris, in Family Guy he also voices the likes of Neil Goldman and various other characters. He is the co-creator and one of the main driving forces behind Robot Chicken. Seth Green also been seen in movies such as America's Sweethearts, Without A Paddle, Rat Race, Scooby Doo 2, The Italian Job and Old Dogs.

SETH FACTS

* When he auditioned for Family Guy, he did an impression of Buffalo Bill from Silence Of The Lambs.
* He was born in Philadelphia.
* Seth is the co-creator of a comic book called Freshmen.

Mila Kunis

VOICES: Meg

Mila Kunis, who voices Meg in Family Guy, was born in the USSR, in Chernivtsi, which is now part of the Ukraine. Her family moved to LA when she was seven, partly to escape the anti-Semitism they'd experienced in her homeland.

She started acting not long after, scoring several small TV roles. She had her first big success with the sitcom That '70s Show, in which she played Jackie Burkhart. She shouldn't really have got the role, as all those who auditioned were supposed to be 18. Even though she was only 14, Kunis tried out for the series anyway. After producers discovered her real age, they still felt she was the best person for the part.

Meg was originally voiced by Lacey Chabert (of Party Of Five fame), but she decided to leave and so a new actress was needed. After auditioning numerous actresses, they settled on Kunis, who took over the role in the Season 2 episode, 'A Picture Is Worth A 1,000 Bucks'. She has been with the show ever since.

MILA FACTS

* Mila is short for Milena.
* Used to date 'Home Alone' star Macaulay Culkin.
* Has different coloured eyes, one blue and one green.

THE OTHER VOICES OF FAMILY GUY

HERE ARE SOME OF THE OTHER VOICES YOU CAN HEAR ON FAMILY GUY

DANNY SMITH
VOICES INCLUDE:
The Giant Chicken, Evil Monkey

JOHN VIENER
VOICES INCLUDE:
Kyle, Derek Wilcox, New Brian

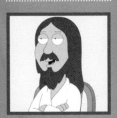

ALEC SULKIN
VOICES INCLUDE:
Jesus, Floyd

LORI ALAN
VOICES INCLUDE:
Diane Simmons

JOHNNY BRENNAN
VOICES INCLUDE:
Mort Goldman, Horace

GARY COLE
VOICES INCLUDE:
Principal Shepard

NICOLE SULLIVAN
VOICES INCLUDE:
Muriel Goldman

JENNIFER TILLY
VOICES INCLUDE:
Bonnie Swanson

CARRIE FISHER
VOICES INCLUDE:
Peter's boss Angela

DREW BARRYMORE
VOICES INCLUDE:
Jillian

CHARLES DURNING
VOICES INCLUDE:
Francis Griffin

JANE LYNCH
VOICES INCLUDE:
Dotty Campbell

ADAM CAROLLA
VOICES INCLUDE:
Death

Mike Henry

VOICES: Herbert

Unlike most of the rest of the Family Guy voice cast, Mike Henry knew Seth MacFarlane long before the TV show began. They first met when Seth was at the Rhode Island School of Design and kept in touch after graduation. When MacFarlane started putting Family Guy together, he phoned Mike and brought him on-board as a writer and voice artist.

Henry tends to voice the characters he created on the show, such as Herbert and Greased Up Deaf Guy. He used to voice Cleveland Brown before that character got its own spin-off show.

MIKE FACTS

* Seth MacFarlane was at the Rhode Island School of Design with Mike's brother, Patrick.
* He's had live-action roles in both Gilmore Girls and Scrubs.

Patrick Warburton

VOICES: Joe

Born in New Jersey, but raised in California, Patrick Warburton is perhaps best known for his big, bass, booming voice, which has been put to good use playing Joe Swanson in Family Guy, ever since the fifth episode when the character was introduced.

He's also appeared in the films Scream 3, The Dish, Men In Black II and Get Smart, while his voice has been used in The Emperor's New Groove, Hoodwinked!, Chicken Little, Open Season, Bee Movie, and Space Chimps. Warburton also voiced Buzz Lightyear in the animated TV show, Buzz Lightyear Of Star Command.

More recently he's been seen playing Jess in the TV sitcom, Rules Of Engagement.

PATRICK FACTS

* Studied marine biology at college, but dropped out to pursue modelling and acting.
* His mother was a little-known actress called Barbara Lord.

EPISODE LIST

EPISODE TITLE	TV SEASON	DVD SEASON
Death Has A Shadow	1	1
I Never Met The Dead Man	1	1
Chitty Chitty Death Bang	1	1
Mind Over Murder	1	1
A Hero Sits Next Door	1	1
The Son Also Draws	1	1
Brian: Portrait Of A Dog	1	1
Peter, Peter, Caviar Eater	2	1
Holy Crap	2	1
Da Boom	2	2
Brian In Love	2	2
Love Thy Trophy	2	1
Death Is A Bitch	2	1
The King Is Dead	2	1
I Am Peter, Hear Me Roar	2	2
If I'm Dyin' I'm Lying'	2	1
Running Mates	2	1
A Picture Is Worth A Thousand Bucks	2	2
Fifteen Minutes Of Shame	2	2
Road To Rhode Island	2	2
Let's Go To The Hop	2	2
Dammit Janet!	2	2
There's Something About Paulie	2	2
He's Too Sexy For His Fat	2	2
E. Peterbus Unum	2	2
The Story On Page One	2	2
Wasted Talent	2	2
Fore Father	2	2
The Thin White Line	3	2

EPISODE TITLE	TV SEASON	DVD SEASON
Brian Does Hollywood	3	3
Mr. Griffin Goes To Washington	3	3
One If By Clam, Two If By Sea	3	3
And The Wiener Is...	3	3
Death Lives	3	3
Lethal Weapons	3	3
Kiss Seen 'Round The World	3	3
Mr. Saturday Knight	3	3
Fish Out Of Water	3	3
Emission Impossible	3	3
To Love And Die In Dixie	3	3
Screwed The Pooch	3	3
Peter Griffin: Husband, Father... Brother?	3	3
Ready, Willing, and Disabled	3	3
A Very Special Family Guy Freakin' Christmas	3	3
Brian Wallows And Peter's Swallows	3	3
From Method To Madness	3	3
Stuck Together, Torn Apart	3	3
European Road Show	3	3
Family Guy Viewer Mail #1	3	3
When You Wish Upon A Weinstein	3	2
North By North Quahog	4	4
Fast Times At Buddy Cianci, Jr. High	4	4
Blind Ambition	4	4
Don't Make Me Over	4	4
The Cleveland-Loretta Quagmire	4	4
Petarded	4	4

EPISODE TITLE	TV SEASON	DVD SEASON
Brian The Bachelor	4	4
8 Simple Rules For Buying My Teenage Daughter	4	4
Breaking Out Is Hard To Do	4	4
Model Misbehavior	4	4
Peter's Got Woods	4	4
The Perfect Castaway	4	4
Jungle Love	4	4
PTV	4	5
Brian Goes Back To College	4	5
The Courtship Of Stewie's Father	4	5
The Fat Guy Strangler	4	5
The Father, The Son, And The Holy Fonz	4	5
Brian Sings And Swings	4	5
Patriot Games	4	5
I Take Thee, Quagmire	4	5
Sibling Rivalry	4	5
Deep Throats	4	5
Peterotica	4	5
You May Now Kiss The... Uh... Guy Who Receives	4	5
Petergeist	4	5
Untitled Griffin Family History	4	5
Stewie B Goode	4	*
Bango Was His Name, Oh!	4	*
Stu And Stewie's Excellent Adventure	4	*
Stewie Love Lois	5	6
Mother Tucker	5	6
Hell Comes To Quahog	5	6
Saving Private Brian	5	6

It's been more than a decade since we first met the Griffins, and since then they've entertained us with over 150 episodes of nutty madness. Have you seen them all? It's also worth knowing that the seasons of Family Guys as they were seen on TV don't quite match the seasons on DVD, so take a look below to see which TV and DVD seasons all the regular episodes of Family Guy feature in, and tick off the episodes you've seen.

EPISODE TITLE	TV SEASON	DVD SEASON
Whistle While You Wife Works	5	6
Prick Up your Ears	5	6
Chick Cancer	5	6
Barely Legal	5	6
Road To Rupert	5	6
Peter's Two Dads	5	6
The Tan Aquatic With Steve Zissou	5	6
Airport '07	5	6
Peter And Bill's Bogus Journey	5	6
No Meals On Wheels	5	7
Boys Do Cry	5	7
No Chris Left behind	5	7
It Takes A Village Idiot (And I Married One)	5	7
Meet The Quagmires	5	7
Blue Harvest	6	**
Movin' Out (Brian's Song)	6	7
Believe It Or Not, Joe's Walking On Air	6	7
Stewie Kills Lois	6	7
Lois Kills Stewie	6	7
Padre De Familia	6	7
Peter's Daughter	6	7
McStroke	6	7
Back To The Woods	6	8
Play It Again, Brian	6	8
The Former Life Of Brian	6	8
Love John Peter	6	8
Love, Blactually	7	8
I Dream Of Jesus	7	8

EPISODE TITLE	TV SEASON	DVD SEASON
Road To Germany	7	8
Baby Not On Board	7	8
The Man With Two Brians	7	8
Tales Of A Third Grade Nothing	7	8
Ocean's Three and a Half	7	8
Family Gay	7	8
The Juice Is Loose	7	8
FOX-y Lady	7	9
Not All Dogs Go to heaven	7	9
420	7	9
Stew-Roids	7	9
We Love You, Conrad	7	9
Three Kings	7	9
Peter's Progress	7	9
Road To The Mutiverse	8	9
Family Goy	8	9
Spies Reminiscent Of Us	8	9
Brain's Go A Brand New Bag	8	9
Hannah Banana	8	9
Quagmire's Baby	8	9
Jerome Is The New Black	8	9
Dog Gone	8	9
Business Guy	8	10
Big Man On Hippocampus	8	10
Dial Meg For Murder	8	10
Extra Large Medium	8	10
Go, Stewie, Go!	8	10
Peter-assment	8	10
Brian Griffin's House Of Payne	8	10

EPISODE TITLE	TV SEASON	DVD SEASON
April In Quahog	8	10
Brian & Stewie	8	10
Quagmire's Dad	8	10
The Splendid Source	8	10
Partial Terms Of Endearment	8	10
Something, Something, Something Dark Side	8	**
And Then There Were Fewer	9	10
Excellence In Broadcasting	9	10
Welcome Back, Carter	9	10
Halloween On Spooner Street	9	
Baby, You Knock Me Out	9	
Brian Writes A Bestseller	9	
Road To The North pole	9	
New Kidney In Town	9	
And I'm Joyce Kinney	9	
Friends Of Peter G.	9	
German Guy	9	
The Hand That Rocks The Wheelchair	9	
Trading Places	9	
Tiegs For Two	9	
Brothers & Sisters	9	
The Big Bang Theory	9	
Foreign Affairs	9	
It's A Trap!	9	**

* Released on DVD as Stewie Griffin: The Untold Story

** Released separately on DVD

123

THE ULTIMATE Family Guy QUIZ

PART 4

1. What is the name of Peter's biological father, as revealed in 'Peter's Two Dads'?

2. Which former US president does Lois, and later Peter, sleep with in 'Bill & Peter's Bogus Journey'?

3. What's the name of the robot formed out of wheelchair users, which Joe uses to attack Peter's restaurant in 'No Meals On Wheel'?

4. When Stewie has to disguise himself as a girl in Texas, due to Quahog thinking he's possessed by the devil, what name does he go by?

5. After Chris gets expelled from James Woods High in 'No Chris Left Behind', what incredibly posh school does his grandfather, Carter, help him get into?

6. Which 1980s film actress does Peter end up married to, after altering the past in the episode 'Meet The Quagmires'?

7. Which convenience store manager is first seen in the episode 'Moving Out (Brian's Song)'?

8. In 'Believe It or Not, Joe's Walking on Air', what operation allows Joe to walk again?

9. In the episode 'Lois Kills Stewie', who actually does kill Stewie after he takes over America?

10. What causes Peter to have a debilitating stroke in the episode 'McStroke'?

11. In the episode 'The Former Life Of Brian', what doesn't make sense about Brian having a 13-year-old son, which is even pointed out in the episode?

12. Which husky voiced character made her last regular appearance in the episode 'Love Blactually', before she died?

We're already 75 questions into the Ultimate Family Guy Quiz, and now they are definitely getting harder! By this point you're probably wondering how the Griffins could have got up to so many shenanigans! It's not over yet...

13. Which main character does not appear for the first time, in the episode above?

14. What surprising person does Peter discover working in Quahog's Dead Formats Records store?

15. After being left home alone in 'Baby Not On Board', where does Stewie get a job in order to try and support himself?

16. In the same episode, Cleveland mentions what about his future for the first time?

17. What's the name of the Griffins perfect, neckscarf-wearing new dog in 'The Man with Two Brians'?

18. Who do the guys decide to rob, in order to pay the medical bills for the birth of Joe's daughter, Susie?

19. In 'Family Gay', Peter does medical tests that involve things such as him getting the squirrel gene, the gay gene and a gene for which famous actor?

20. Which controversial former murder suspect does Peter befriend in the episode 'The Juice Is Loose'?

21. In 'FOX-y Lady', filmmaker Michael Moore and conservative TV host Rush Limbaugh are both revealed to be which former child star?

22. Stewie manages to bring together the entire cast of which sci-fi show in the episode 'Not All Dogs Go To Heaven'?

23. The episode 'Three Kings' is made up of parodies of three stories by which famed horror author?

24. Why didn't Lois know her mother was actually Jewish until the episode 'Family Goy'?

25. Animated versions of which two 1980s films stars discover Mayor West is actually a KGB sleeper agent in the episode, 'Spies Reminiscent of Us'?

TURN TO PAGE 140 FOR THE ANSWERS

HIGHTLIGHTS

 The Man With Two Brians

After being injured trying to save Peter, the Griffins get worried that their dog, Brian, is getting old and may die soon.

Their solution is to buy another dog, New Brian, who makes the old Brian feel like an outcast, as he seems so perfect. Brian decides to move out.

One person not fooled by New Brian though is Stewie, who becomes increasingly aggravated by the new dog's cheerfulness, helpfulness and folksy wisdom. When Stewie tries to convince New Brian to leave, he discovers the dog has a dark side, which includes violating Stewie's beloved teddy, Rupert.

New Brian doesn't realise that Stewie is not a baby to be messed with!

TOP MOMENT: PETER AND HIS FRIENDS TRYING TO RECREATE JACKASS STUNTS.

TOP QUOTE: "WELL, RUPERT SEEMS TO LIKE MY HUMPING... HUMPED HIM FOR TWO HOURS YESTERDAY. HE JUST LAID THERE AND TOOK IT." NEW BRIAN

 Family Gay

Peter buys a brain-damaged horse that causes lots of damage when it goes on a rampage during a race. The horse then dies and Peter throws it through the window of Goldman's Pharmacy to get rid of it.

Peter needs money to pay for the damage the horse has caused and decides to join some paid medical experiments, once of which ends up with him being injected with the gay gene.

Lois isn't sure what to think about her hubby being gay, and while warming to his new, more sensitive side, she isn't impressed by him rejecting her sexual advances.

Things get worse when Peter meets a man and leaves Lois for him. Realising how distraught Lois is, Stewie and Brian decide to kidnap Peter and convert him back to heterosexuality.

TOP MOMENT: PETER PREPARING FOR AN 11-WAY GAY ORGY, BUT HAVING A CHANGE OF HEART JUST AS IT'S ABOUT TO BEGIN.

TOP QUOTE: "I'M HERE, I'M QUEER, BUT DON'T GET USED TO IT 'CAUSE I'M LEAVING YOU!" PETER

3 Stew-Roids

Ashamed of him being beaten up by a female baby, Peter takes Stewie to the Quahog Boxing Gym to learn how to be a man.

He's given some steroids to help make Stewie more ripped. The baby takes them and becomes incredibly buff, enjoying his new body as it allows him to boss Brian around. When the steroids wear off, Stewie has too much skin!

Chris finds unexpected popularity when he begins dating Connie DiMico, who's run out of genuinely cool people to date. After initially falling for Connie

and making her realise perhaps she's been wrong about boys, his new status starts to go to his head, breaking Connie's heart when he starts flirting with other women. An unexpected alliance is formed when Connie and Meg get together to bring Chris down a peg or two.

TOP MOMENT: CHRIS RE-ENACTING THE 'TUCK IT BETWEEN YOUR LEGS' MOMENT FROM SILENCE OF THE LAMBS.

TOP QUOTE: "WHAT WAS WEIRD WAS THAT SHE WAS CRYING, BUT THE WAY SHE WAS STANDING OVER ME MADE IT LOOK LIKE I WAS CRYING, WHICH WAS WEIRD." STEWIE

QUAGMIRE'S DAD

Quagmire is excited because his father, a decorated naval hero, is coming to visit. Despite Glen's insistence that his pops is legendary with the ladies, the guys can't help but feel Dan is a bit gay.

They confront Glen about this, and while Quagmire is adamant they're wrong, he ends up asking his father anyway, only to discover his dad isn't gay, but does intend to get a sex-change operation while he's in town.

Dan becomes Ida, and while Quagmire does his best to deal with this drastic change, the pair end up having a huge argument about what's happened. Things move up a gear when Brian meets Ida in a hotel bar and ends up in her hotel room, sharing a bed for the night.

TOP MOMENT: BRIAN THROWING UP FOR 30 SECONDS AFTER DISCOVERING IDA'S TRUE IDENTITY

TOP QUOTE: "I F**KED YOUR DAD!" BRIAN

2 Go, Stewie, Go!

Stewie discovers they're planning to make a US version of Jolly Farm Revue, and decides to audition.

But they only want little girls! Stewie disguises himself as 'Karina Smirnoff' and gets a job on the show. He soon becomes smitten with co-star Julie, who believes Stewie is a girl too!

Meg gets a new boyfriend called Anthony, who shocks Lois by being normal and attractive. Already feeling insecure about

aging, Lois makes a move on Anthony, and Meg discovers them making out on the couch!

TOP MOMENT: STEWIE HAVING TO CHANGE FROM HIMSELF TO KARINA, WHILE NOT ALLOWING JULIE TO REALISE THEY'RE ACTUALLY THE SAME PERSON.

TOP QUOTE: "BRIAN, WE BOTH KNOW I TOUCHED IT. NOW, IF YOU'D LIKE TO KEEP THAT JUST BETWEEN US, I SUGGEST YOU SIT BACK DOWN AND ORDER ME SOME CHICKEN FINGERS." STEWIE

WHAT'S THE WORD?

THE BEST QUOTES OF BRIAN GRIFFIN

STEWIE: I mean, what kind of man would I be if I ran off now?

BRIAN: Well, you would be a black man.

STEWIE: Whoa, whoa, whoa, what was that?

BRIAN: Ah, I'm sorry, I'm sorry. That was my father talking.

STEWIE: You, uh, gotta work on that man. Bad dog.

From: Chick Cancer

"You know, Peter, I hate to say 'I told you so' about you not being a genius, but... IN YOUR F**KING FACE, F**KWAD!... I, I'm sorry about that."

From: Petarded

(TO PETER) "BOY, IT'S AMAZING, ISN'T IT? YOU GET TWO FATHERS, AND NEITHER ONE OF THEM WANTS ANYTHING TO DO WITH YOU."

From: Peter's Two Dads

STEWIE: [imitating Brian] I'm the dog! I'm well-read and have a diverse stock portfolio, but I'm not above eating grass clippings and regurgitating them on the small braided rug near the door.

BRIAN: [imitating Stewie] I'm a pompous little Antichrist who will probably abandon my plans for world domination when I grow up and fall in love with a rough trick named Jim.

From: Lethal Weapons

STEWIE: How can you have a 13-year-old son when you're only 7?

BRIAN: Those are dog years.

STEWIE: That doesn't make any sense.

BRIAN: You know what, Stewie? If you don't like it, go on the internet and complain.

From: The Former Life Of Brian

"I DON'T KNOW. I GUESS TAKING CARE OF THIS OLD WOMAN WILL BE JUST LIKE BABYSITTING, ONLY WITH BIGGER DIAPERS."

From: Brian Swallows and Peter's Swallows

BRIAN: This sucks! I can't believe that judge is making us go to a month of AA.

LOIS: You know, if you ask me, this is going to be a good thing for both of you. There's a lesson you need to learn.

BRIAN: What are you talking about? What lesson? I don't need to go to AA. I'm a social drinker, not an alcoholic.

STEWIE: Pfff! Yeah, that's like saying rappers are really poets.

From: Friends Of Peter G

BRIAN: Now insert tab A into slot B.

PETER: That's what sh...

BRIAN: If you say, "That's what she said" one more time, I'm gonna pop you.

From: Emission Impossible

LOIS: [commenting on Peter's new moustache] I think it's handsome.

BRIAN: I think it's gay.

PETER: Oh yeah? Well, if I'm gay then Freddie Mercury was gay.

BRIAN: Freddie Mercury, the lead singer of Queen? He was incredibly gay!

PETER: He was not. He had a moustache. That's practically like having a wedding band.

From: McStroke

STEWIE: WELL, ALL'S WELL THAT ENDS WELL, EH, BRIAN?

BRIAN: YOU SHOT ME IN BOTH LEGS AND LIT ME ON FIRE. PISS OFF.

From: Patriot Games

"IF DOGS AREN'T SUPPOSED TO EAT DENTAL FLOSS OUT OF THE TRASH, WHY DID THEY MAKE IT MINT FLAVOURED?"

From: Fast Times At Buddy Cianci High

BRIAN: Hey, do you hear that?

PETER: What?

BRIAN: Sounds like someone's screaming.

PETER: What... What is it boy? What are you trying to say?

BRIAN: It sounds like Loretta is screaming.

PETER: Trouble at the old mill?

BRIAN: What, are you insane?

PETER: Somebody fall through the ice?

BRIAN: It's summer.

PETER: Bobcat?

BRIAN: Woof, woof, woof, woof, woof, woof.

PETER: Loretta's in trouble? Come on boy!

From: The Cleveland-Loretta Quagmire

The Griffin Family Tree

"DON'T THANK ME, LOIS, THANK MY ANCESTORS FOR LIVING LIVES OF GREATNESS."

THE GRIFFINS HAVE A LONG AND ILLUSTRIOUS HISTORY. FROM PRETTY MUCH THE BEGINNING OF TIME, PETER'S RELATIVES HAVE BEEN GETTING UP TO STRANGE AND INCREDIBLE ANTICS. HERE ARE JUST A FEW OF THEM...

Ur-Peter

The earliest known Griffin relative was a caveman, often known as Ur-Peter. He invented the wheel but had trouble selling it, as everyone was too excited about the trapezoid. Luckily Ur-Brian realises that the best way to market something is to use sex. Making Ur-Lois parade about in a fur bikini certainly helped sales.

Moses Griffin

Someone had to lead the Israelites out of Egypt, and turns out it was Moses Griffin, Peter's ancient ancestor. His ten commandments aren't quite the same as the ones in the Bible, instead insisting: "Commandment #1 – Shut the hell up. Commandment #2 – There's nothing I can do about the sun. Commandment #3 – There are no more Jolly Ranchers, they're all gone. Commandment #4 – When we pass a billboard, please don't read it out loud."

Peter Hitler

Yes, believe it or not, Peter is related to Hitler… or at least his brother! Peter Hitler often annoyed his brother, Adolf, when he was busy doing 'Nazi Stuff'. He did do the world a big favour by accidentally shooting both Adolf and Eva Braun, and then making it look like a suicide pact.

Angus Griffin

Peter's centuries old Scottish ancestor is one of the inventors of golf. At the game's inception he claimed black people or Jews shouldn't play the game.

Juarez Griffin

A rather strange, diminutive Mexican great grandfather of Peter. He's so small that he was a professional cockfighter who beat up chickens.

Huck Griffin

It would appear that one of Peter's ancestors inspired Mark Twain's Huckleberry Finn. Unlike in the book, he's not allowed to use racial slurs when he refers to his friend, Jim, and so has to find a PC way around things.

Nate Griffin

Peter's great-great-great-great grandfather wasn't just black, he was a slave owned by Lois's ancestors, The Pewterschmidts. Brought from Africa against his will (he was born in Quahogswana), Nate was put to work on the Pewterschmidt's plantation, but had sex (and kids) with the beautiful Lois Laura Bush Lynne Cheney Pewterschmidt – and her sister!

Rufus Griffin

Another black relative was Peter's cousin, Rufus Griffin. He became a famous star of Blaxploitation movies such as 'Caddyblack', 'Blackdraft' and 'Black To The Future'.

Thaddeus Griffin

Peter's evil twin has only been mentioned once, but he is the stereotypical villain, with a waxed moustache to twirl and a cape. He often wonders how his inheritance will be affected.

Ulysses S. Griffin

Ulysses is the man who ended the Civil War. However he didn't do it on the battlefield – but put an ending to the South's secession by beating Robert E. Lee in a drinking contest.

Ponce De Leon Griffin

A medieval explorer, Ponce De Leon Griffin was desperate to find the Fountain of Youth. Miraculously he was successful in his quest, but when he jumped in the Fountain up to his neck, he came out with his head the same age but the body of a baby. Not the result he was hoping for!

Josiah Griffin

Peter's grandfather helped to create Bugs Bunny as one of the animators working at Warner Bros. While they were trying to work out what to call the character, Josiah lobbied for 'Ephraim The Retarded Rabbit'. He was overruled.

Griffin Peterson

The most important man in the history of Quahog! Exiled to America by King Stewart after falling for Lady Redbush, Griffin was Quahog's founder. He declared: "We're gonna build a new settlement. We'll have a happy new life, and we'll have equal rights for all. Except Blacks, Asians, Hispanics, Jews, gays, women, Muslims, um, everybody who's not a white man. And I mean 'white' white, so no Italians, no Polish. Just people from Ireland, England, and Scotland. But from only certain parts of Scotland and Ireland. Just full-blooded whites. No, y'know what? Not even whites. Nobody gets any rights. Ahhhh… America."

STEWIE MAY NEVER SEEM TO AGE, BUT ONCE YOU'RE DEAD YOU'RE DEAD. SAY GOODBYE TO SOME FAMILY GUY FRIENDS WHO DIDN'T SURVIVE SEASON 9.

Family Guy
Obituaries

✝ Muriel Goldman

Wife of Mort and mother of Neil, the ridiculously Jewish Muriel meets an ignominious end in the episode 'And Then There Were Fewer'. She is the victim of a killer who cuts a swathe through the Quahog residents who are invited to a dinner hosted by James Woods.

Muriel is found dead with a knife in her back, having surprised the killer and paid the ultimate price. However even in her death, her husband found it difficult to find anything too great to say about her. His immediate eulogy was:

"Oh, my God, Muriel! My sweet Muriel! She was so youn... She was so beauti... She was so genero... Uh, we were married."

✝ Derek Wilcox

It's good news for Brian when Derek Wilcox gets hit with a Golden Globe Award and falls from a balcony, as it removes the main obstacle from him trying to get back with his great love, Jillian.

Derek was Jillian's husband, a man who was almost ridiculously perfect, even if he was a tad patronising to his moronic wife.

Fluent in both French and Mandarin Chinese, able to fix broken elbows and very well endowed (and according to Peter, able to hold up the Hollywood sign single-handedly), Wilcox was such a super-person that he really annoyed Brian. Wilcox and Jillian married despite Brian's attempt to stop the wedding.

✝ Diane Simmons

The perky female anchor of Channel 5 News is shot and falls off a cliff. That seems like a pretty definitive way to go (although you never know!). Simmons had hosted the news alongside Tom Tucker since Family Guy began, always ready with a chipper word, even if she and Tom did like to bicker. At one point Simmons burst into tears on air when Tucker pointed out how her first husband blew his brains out.

She was certainly not perfect and once admitted that "I just plain don't like black people". She also stole the lead in a production of 'The King & I' from Loretta Brown. Diane had recently turned 40 when she died.

THE ULTIMATE Family guy quiz

PART 5

1. What surprising secret do Stewie and Brian discover about Hannah Montana/Miley Cyrus in 'Hannah Banana'?

2. In 'Quagmire's Baby', what is the name of the daughter Glen discovers he has?

3. What's the name of the new 'black guy' Peter finds to replace Cleveland, but who he decides he doesn't like when he discovers his new friend once slept with Lois?

4. What TV talk show do the Griffins appear on in the episode 'Big Man On Hippocampus', with Peter completely losing his memory by the end of the taping?

5. In the episode 'Extra Large Medium', why does Joe think Peter might be able to help him find a missing person who has a bomb tied to them?

6. Who provides the voice of Peter's Pawtucket Patriot manager, Angela?

7. In the episode 'Brian Griffin's House Of Payne', what name does James Woods insist Brian's TV show, 'What I Learned on Jefferson Street', is changed to?

8. What astronomical event do the citizens of Quahog believe is going to cause the end of the world, in the episode 'April In Quahog'?

9. When Quagmire's dad, Dan, comes to town and announces he's going to have a sex change, what name does he want to go by as a woman?

10. Why was the episode 'Partial Terms Of Endearment', in which Lois agrees to be a surrogate mother, first screened on TV in the UK rather than the US?

11. In the murder-mystery Season 9 opener, 'And Then There Were Fewer', who turned out to be the actual killer of Muriel Goldman, Derek Wilcox and others?

12. And who killed that killer?

And now, the end is here. Well, almost! It's your last chance to prove to the world that you're almost an honorary resident of Quahog. This final section includes five particularly fiendish posers only the most obsessed Family Guy fan will know the answers to!

13. In 'Halloween On Spooner Street', what does Quagmire claim his grandfather was during the Second World War?

14. In the same episode, it's revealed that Quagmire was the first person to have what disease?

15. In 'Brian Writes A Bestseller', what is the name of the self-help book that Brian writes?

16. And what was the name of the novel Brian was working on for years, but which hardly sold any copies when it was published?

17. Who eventually donates a kidney to Peter in order to save his life in the Season 9 episode 'New Kidney in Town'?

18. In the episode 'Friends Of Peter G', what reason is revealed for why weather forecaster Ollie Williams only speaks in shouted, incredibly short sentences?

19. What's the name of the blue movie Lois is exposed for having appeared in, in the episode 'And I'm Joyce Kinney'?

20. Including her new marriage to Mayor West, how many people has Lois's sister Carol been married to?

...and now five fiendishly difficult questions...

21. What's the name of the mansion the Griffins inherit in the episode, 'Peter, Peter, Caviar Eater'?

22. What's the theme of the floats in the annual Harvest Festival parade in the episode, 'Love Thy Trophy'?

23. In 'Lethal Weapons', what is the name of Lois' Tae-Jitsu Master?

24. Who recorded Peterotica on tape?

25. What was the first line of dialogue spoken in the first ever episode of Family Guy, 'Death Has A Shadow'?

TURN TO PAGE 140 FOR THE ANSWERS

WHAT'S THE WORD?

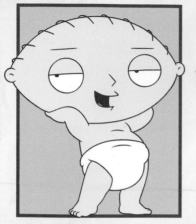

THE BEST QUOTES OF STEWIE GRIFFIN

LOIS: What are you kids doing?

STEWIE: Playing 'House'.

LOIS: But the kid is tied up in the basement.

STEWIE: ...Roman Polanski's house.

From: The Kiss Seen Around The World

PETER: Hey, Lois, did you say something?

LOIS: Oh, just that I think you're gonna love this cake.

STEWIE: (Dressed as a girl) None for me, thanks. It's gonna go straight to my vagina. That's what girls worry about, right? Having big vaginas?

From: Boys Do Cry

BRIAN: So what happened?

STEWIE: Well, you wanna know what I learned this week? Being a grown-up sucks. Women, Brian, what a royal pain in the ass. It's like, it's like why can't you just hang out with guys, you know, just live with someone of your own sex, just do what you do with women, but with your buddy. You know what, why don't guys just do that?

BRIAN: They do. It's called being gay.

STEWIE: Oh, is that what gay is? Oh, yeah. I could totally get into that.

From: Chick Cancer

CHRIS: Hey, birthday dude! You want some ice cream?

STEWIE: Yes, but no sprinkles. For every sprinkle I find, I shall kill you.

From: Chitty Chitty Death Bang

"Damn you, vile woman! You've impeded my work since the day I escaped from your wretched womb."

From: Death Has A Shadow

BRIAN: Listen kid there's something I've been meaning to tell you. It's not easy for me to say.

STEWIE: Oh god, you're not coming out of the closet are you? Ugh, why does everyone always come out to me?

From: Road To Rhode Island

"Come on, discipline me! Make me wear panties, rub dirt in my eye, violate me with a wine bottle! My God, I really do have problems, don't I?"

From: Peter's Two Dads

STEWIE: You need more than that. You need an act. Listen, I'll be your assistant and we'll put on a whole big show.

BRIAN: Really?

STEWIE: Yeah. We'll do all the great tricks. You can even split me in half.

BRIAN: What?

STEWIE: Saw me in half.

From: The Former Life Of Brian

"God, all this work keeping people from having sex. Now I know how the Catholic Church feels!"

From: Emission Impossible

"Damn you, ice cream! Come to my mouth! How dare you disobey me!"

From: He's Too Sexy For His Fat

"HEAVENS, IT APPEARS MY WEE-WEE HAS BEEN STRICKEN WITH RIGOR MORTIS."

From: Peter Griffin: Husband, Father... Brother?

"WHAT ARE THESE? PANCAKES? OH, OH, THESE ARE DELECTABLE. GOOD NEWS FLAPPY, I'VE DECIDED NOT TO KILL YOU!"

From: Love The Trophy

LOIS: Look, Stewie, a note. You know, Mommy doesn't usually read things out of Chris' pocket. She's more respectful than that.

STEWIE: Yeah, whatever helps you sleep at night, bitch.

From: Fast Times At Buddy Cianci Jr. High

"YOU CALL THOSE CHEAP IMPLANTS "BOOBS"? THEY'RE LIES!"

From: I Take Thee, Quagmire

"Easy! Massage the scalp. You're washing a baby's hair, not scrubbing vomit off your Christmas dress, you holiday drunk."

From: Brian Does Hollywood

"Aha! So they do make bigger diapers! That deceitful woman told me I'd have to learn to use the toilet! Well, fie on the toilet! It's made slaves of you all! I've seen it sitting in there - lazy, slothful, porcelain layabout feeding on other people's doo-doos while contributing nothing of its own to society!"

From: Brian Wallows And Peter's Swallows

"I'D LOVE TO STAY AND CHAT, BUT YOU'RE A TOTAL BITCH."

From: From Method To Madness

"YOU WILL NOT CALL THEM MOMMY AND DADDY! IT'S LOIS AND THE FAT MAN, DO YOU UNDERSTAND ME?"

From: Stu & Stewie's Excellent Adventure

"There's always been a lot of tension between Lois and me, and it's not so much that I want to kill her, it's just, I want her to not be alive anymore."

From: Fifteen Minutes Of Shame

Goodbye

FROM SPOONER STREET

AND NOW, THE END IS HERE... WELL, THE END OF THIS BOOK ANYWAY. BUT DON'T WORRY, DEATH AND HIS DOG SHOULDN'T BE KNOCKING ON YOUR DOOR ANY MOMENT NOW!

not your normal family – after all, not many people have a father who needed a new kidney after an energy drink experiment went awry, or a mother with a past in porn – but it's certainly true life is more fun when they're around.

And who knows what will happen next! Will Mayor West's marriage to Lois' sister succeed? Will Quagmire ever get back with Cheryl Tiegs?

Will Bonnie get itchy feet once more and want to leave Joe? Is it really the end of Bertram? Will Brian find love? Will realising he's responsible for the creation of the universe go to Stewie's head?

Who knows? But there's little doubt it's going to be fun finding out.

We can give you a hint at what's coming in Season 10 though, such as that the Griffins struggle to stay grounded after winning the lottery, Meg falls for an Amish boy and Stewie gets behind the wheel to take the family car for a spin.

Then, on Meg's 18th birthday, Quagmire moves in for the kill and Peter tries to put an end to the relationship. Plus everything comes full circle when Brian and Stewie travel back in time to the very first episode of the series! And that's just some of the treats in store!

So it's goodbye from Peter, Lois, Chris, Meg, Stewie, Joe, Quagmire, Herbert, Mort, Mayor West, Tom Tucker and even the Giant Chicken, until their next load of eccentric tomfoolery descends upon us.

It's time to say goodbye to the residents of Spooner Street and their anarchic adventures, while we wait for even more nuttiness coming our way in Season 10!

Don't panic though, Peter's still technically retarded, Lois is still one sexy mama, Chris remains dumb as a box of rock, Stewie continues being evil and Meg is, well, ugly.

You can be certain too that Joe is still clearing the streets of bad guys, Herbert's trying and failing to attract young boys and Glen is chasing every skirt within a 100 mile radius (giggity).

Season 9 was quite an adventure, taking in everything from Chris and Meg's incest to the near-death of Santa. The episodes were yet more proof that the Griffins are

GOODBYE – AND AS PETER WOULD SAY, "SHUT UP, MEG!"

ANSWERS

THE ULTIMATE FAMILY GUY QUIZ ANSWERS

PART 1

1. 1999
2. Death Has A Shadow
3. Season 7
4. Jesse
5. He electrocuted himself in the bath, having borrowed Peter's toaster for the job
6. Christobel
7. Aunt Marguerite
8. Because it has a Twinkie factory, supposedly the only food that can survive a nuclear war
9. The King & I
10. Gumbel 2 Gumbel Beach Justice
11. He was a weather mime
12. The Real Live Griffins
13. Tom Arnold and Fran Drescher
14. Mayor West
15. Biscuit
16. Dylan
17. The Quahog Beautiful People's Club
18. Petoria
19. Luke Perry
20. Pawtucket Pat
21. He's gets addicted to drugs and has to go to rehab
22. Porn movies
23. El Dorado Cigarette Company
24. Nigel Pinchley
25. Peter Frampton

PART 2

1. Kevin
2. He chokes on a dinner roll while having dinner with the Griffins
3. Renaissance Fair Jouster
4. Daggermouth
5. Bumblescum
6. A pig called Oinky
7. Sea Breeze
8. Get neutered
9. Nate Griffin
10. Kichwa Tembo
11. Bea Arthur
12. Plutonium
13. The paper towels have run out
14. Pearl Burton
15. He has to look after her as part of his community service for a drink driving offence
16. The Campbells
17. Olivia
18. Mort and Muriel Goldman
19. The pianio
20. Jolly Farm Revue
21. KISS-stock
22. A camel
23. To see what TV host Kelly Ripa is like off-camera, to have his own theme music, and to have no bones
24. She can grow her fingernails at will
25. He thinks it will automatically make Chris do better at school

PART 3

1. Passion Of The Christ 2: Crucify This
2. It was a conspiracy between Mrs. Lockhart and a talking bear
3. Swallowing the most nickels
4. Saturday Night Live
5. Glen Quagmire
6. Cleveland Brown
7. Doug
8. Mystique from X-Men
9. Asiantown
10. Martin Luther King
11. Brown
12. Patrick
13. Robert Downey Jr.
14. Frank Sinatra Jr.
15. The London Sillinannies
16. Joan
17. Hand Full Of Peter
18. Jasper
19. A prostate exam
20. It was the name of Stewie and Brian's radio show
21. Peter destroying Cleveland's house, causing him and his bath to drop onto the lawn
22. Splash Log
23. Ear Sex
24. Steel Vaginas
25. Because South America isn't wheelchair accessible

PART 4

1. Mickey McFinnigan
2. Bill Clinton
3. Crippletron
4. Stephanie Griffin
5. Morningwood Academy
6. Molly Ringwald
7. Carl
8. A leg transplant
9. Peter
10. Eating 30 hamburgers in a row
11. Brian is only seven years old
12. Loretta Brown
13. Chris
14. Jesus
15. McBurgertown
16. He tells Quagmire he's